Teacher Training

Eloisa de Oliveira Lima

Teacher Training

*Forewords by
Patrícia Corsino
Louise Brown
Margarita Vega*

*Ibis Libris
Rio de Janeiro
2018*

Copyright © 2018 Eloisa de Oliveira Lima

Publisher: Thereza Christina Rocque da Motta
Interior and cover design: Sergio Pereira (sergio@novidea.com.br)
Contribution: José Mauro Pinheiro/UFRJ

1st Edition October 2018.

Lima, Eloisa de Oliveira, 1953-
    How to acquire a second language : from the beginning of speech / Eloisa de Oliveira Lima ; forewords by Louise Brown, Margarita Vega, Patrícia Corsino. – Rio de Janeiro : Ibis Libris, 2018.
    144 p. ; 21cm.

    ISBN 978-85-7823-321-1

    1. English language – Study and teaching – Methodology 2. English language – Foreign speakers – Study and teaching I. Título II. Brown, Louise II. Vega, Margarita III. Corsino, Patrícia

CDD 428.24

1. English language – Study and teaching – Methodology

Author's e-mail: eloisalima@me.com

All rights reserved.

2018

Ibis Libris Editora Ltda.
Rua Pereira Nunes, 396 / 1.701
Vila Isabel – Rio de Janeiro – RJ
Brazil
20.541-022

+ 55 21 | 3546-1007

ibislibris.loja2.com.br
ibislibris@gmail.com

A member of LIBRE.
www.libre.org.br

TABLE OF CONTENTS

7	Dedications
9	Acknowlegdments
11	Foreword I, by Patrícia Corsino
14	Foreword II, by Louise Brown
16	Foreword III, by Margarita Vega
	PART I
17	A) Author's Note
19	B) Constructivism: Usage and Perspectives in Education
22	C) The Epistemologist and the Pedagogue: Jean Piaget and Lauro de Oliveira Lima
26	D) The Piagetian Teacher
31	E) Comments on Existing Methods Employed in the Teaching of a Foreign Language
35	F) The Stages of Mental Development: A Description of Mental Levels according to the Psychogenetic Theory
46	G) How to Develop the Language of Children
49	H) Development of Reading – Literacy: Know How
55	I) Very Important Explanatory Vocabulary related to Piagetian Notions employed in Psychopedagogical Methodology
	PART 2
61	A) How to Plan an English Class in terms of the Piagetian Approach
75	B) The Classification of the Universe
91	C) The Syllabus
100	D) Suggested Activities as part of this following Methodology

129	E) Techniques and Advice for the Teacher Towards Students' Dynamics
134	F) Evaluation of the Students in terms of the Clinical Method
141	Conclusion
143	Bibliography

DEDICATIONS

*"There's no Genesis without structure,
nor structure without genesis".*
Jean Piaget

Thus, I dedicate this work to the CHILD of the world who has been subject to so much comment, so much study and even so, still so misunderstood. In particular, to my only child, Bruno, who has played such an important role in this entire constructive process. Bruno was born in the middle of the embryo stage of this idea, and served as a test, involving different kinds of material. He was a product of my theory of learning a language, having concluded his "time" of studies in a brilliant manner. At the age of eleven years old, he succeeded in passing the University of Cambridge – London – P.E.T. "Preliminary English Test", without ever having lived outside Brazil.

He patiently divided his mother's attention among books and papers for hours on end; always tender, inquiring, showing happiness and enthusiasm.

Thank you my son. I am very proud of you. Thank you, Ricardo, my constant companion, a source of strength and admiration for my work. Many more grateful thanks for making the dream of establishing our study center where this methodology could be put into practice become a reality in several schools.

Thank you for the meeting of our two lives and for the healthy harmony arising there from – the tonus of my journey.

I would also like to say thank you to several teachers who collaborated and were at my side during the preparation of this work, for their extreme efforts of excellence, always exceeded by their daily activities with the children.

Thank you for the willingness and intellectual capacity shown in achieving the goals set with the children – as we call students.

Thanks are also extended to the parents of the children who, as pioneers, believed in this bold concept of teaching languages and trusted us with their works of art – their children since very young age (18 months old up to 12 years old).

I thank my parents for their battle to give me education.

I thank my father in law, Lauro de Oliveira Lima, for all the theoretical and practical possibilities he furnished me in order to face the eternal challenge of life.

ACKNOWLEDGMENTS

I'm thankful for my book.

To the people that I should express gratitude since that without them this book wouldn't exist.

The first person I thank is my husband, Ricardo Lima, for being my right hand side during my entire professional pedagogical journey. There were several readings, suggestions and friendship along several years of work together; without him, this experiment wouldn't exist.

I thank DICE pedagogical staff – the first reason for all this to exist.

I thank Marcio Martins, who has contributed a lot and motivated me looking forward to realizing the Project and turning it all into a book.

Thank you, Mauro Pinheiro, from UFRJ, the strongest person during the construction of the Project. Concise and keen, he has supported me to organize all the data included in the material.

Thank you, Elen, by the careful review of the texts.

I hope this material can contribute to teachers who deal with children since very young age, making them learn a new language with happiness, seriousness and enthusiasm, and always having fun.

FOREWORD I

"How to Acquire a Second Language from the Beginning of Speech" presents a clear format, an objective and consistent design of a method for teaching a foreign language developed by Eloisa Lima. It's the gathering of more than 40 years of a research teacher, who articulates in a singular and authorial way a study of Jean Piaget's psychogenic theory and the pedagogical method developed by Professor Lauro de Oliveira Lima in Jean Piaget's Educational and Experimental Center for learning of a second language for children, starting at a very young age. The challenge of developing a methodology capable of making children speak English without having to go through repetitive exercises or tiresome situations was what made Eloisa dare to search for innovative approaches which could be applied to teaching any language.

The book is organized in two sections. In its first part, the Author exposes the theoretical and methodological assumptions which support the methodology. The Author contextualizes her trajectory as a teacher as well as her pursuit of developing a creative method of teaching a foreign language to children from 1 to 13 years old and Jean Piaget's and Lauro de Oliveira Lima's trajectory.

Two assertives are basic in the proposed learning process: "Each and every learning proposal made to a child should consider the mental level of that child at the time the learning process is conducted"; and "The teacher does not teach: the student is helped to learn". It starts from the principle that being a Piagetian teacher demands a change in the perception of education, a "challenge, criticism, a great deal of determination to create arguments, attempts, tips and hints, options, research sources, the unusual, the new, originality and never supplying the answer."

Another important matter of the proposal is the possibility of leaning a foreign language in real communicative situations, with creative challenges, and problem situations which lead to the pursuit of answers with the involvement of games as a fundamental resource for the children to resolve problems collectively. The methodology considers it necessary to approach the three points which characterize the nature of a language, which are: structural – a language has a structure which gives it a form and it is necessary that children know another linguistic code in order to attribute it to the world around them; functional – any language exercises different social functions; interactional – a language allows us to interact with one another in different situations. The methodology is based in theory and knowledge, the Author expresses that "it has as its general objective the placing of the child in his or her social group. Thus, in presenting a new possibility of expression, we are also contributing to the child's educational process and their capacity to respect the other."

Still in this first part, the Author presents a precise summarized description of the developmental stages according to Jean Piaget's psychogenetic theory, as follows: sensory motor, symbolic, intuitive, operatory concrete and operatory abstract which serve as the basis of the development of pedagogical proposals. It is worth noting that it makes important reservations to the sense that the teacher does not take them in a linear way and does not reduce them to the succinct descriptions which are presented. This care demonstrates the seriousness of the Author in face of a complex theory whose syntheses show its theoretical domain and ability to articulate with the teaching of a foreign language. It is also worth highlighting the Author's analysis of the vocabulary related to the Piagetian psycho-pedagogy, and ends this part by calling teachers to be creative, to do differently, to seek and create new problem situations for children to solve.

In the second part of the book, the Author is generous in making her methodology widely available in full detail. Discussing planning for each stage, materials to be used during the activities, possible assimilation schemes to be considered, as well as examples of activities to be developed and complexified. Objects, stories, cards, CDs, DVDs are all presented as possibilities of a creative and challenging pedagogical proposal. In addition, it presents unit proposals for the development of contextualized work which favors the expansion of children's language skills. All of these exemplify a methodology that proposes many stories, songs, drawings, games, imitations, dramatizations and diverse activities according to the stages of the children, ending with suggestions for evaluating the children.

There is no doubt that we are faced with a daring production that invites foreign-language teachers to observe and to listen to children, to think about their work and their interactions with them, to use their imagination with consistency, to present children with a second language in a challenging and playful manner as yet another way to see and to interact with the world. Eloisa Lima summarizes in her book a methodology that has been sculpted with a lot of dedication, study, observation, seriousness and consistency. A contribution to foreign-language teaching for children from one to thirteen-year-old. Enjoy!

Patrícia Corsino
Associate Professor at the School of Education
and the Graduate Program in Education at UFRJ, BR

FOREWORD II

Eloisa Lima has written an important book that dwells into the philosophy and methodology for teaching a second language to young children beginning at the earliest age. She has dedicated her life to learning and presenting her ideas and methodology to fellow teachers and school administrators.

When Eloisa Lima first discussed her language program with me, I thought it would be enjoyable to meet the Brazilian students who attended her language school. She described how very young children came to her school and began the study of English. When they felt comfortable, the students requested her to bring them to the United States so they might study in an English speaking school. She suggested her students to come and attend classes in my school so they could be immersed in English. I didn't need to be convinced to participate in this experience. Language is the heart of any culture and I felt this would be a great way for all our children to learn about Brazil.

The Brazilian students arrived and were ready to begin classes. They joined the different grade levels according to their ages. Soon they were following along and enjoying the lessons in English with very little hesitancy. They engaged with our students and learned through activities in and out of school. The ease with which the students assimilated into our school is a validation of the teaching methods described in this book.

Friendships were made and memories created that will forever be cherished by everyone. It was a very enriching experience for our teachers, students and our entire learning community.

Eloisa Lima's book reveals her synthesis of the philosophies of Jean Piaget and Professor Lauro de Oliveira Lima upon which she has based her school and her teachings.

Her successes in teaching children can be attributed to the methods that she describes in her book. This is a very thorough and informative book and belongs on the shelf of all teachers. Teaching a language can be challenging and the strategies described herein are useful, relevant, and they really work.

What a joyous privilege to work with Eloisa Lima and watch her students succeed. I observed this inspirational program in action over a period of fifteen years and can truthfully say it was extremely successful.

Louise Brown
Elementary School Principal
Orange County Public School

FOREWORD III

We were fortunate to host Eloisa Lima, her teachers and most importantly, the students, participating in the DICE school from Rio de Janeiro, Brazil. The students were immersed in elementary school classes taught by teachers here in Orange County Public Schools of Orlando, Florida. It was a highly educational program for both the students of Brazil and our students. Bonds of friendship were formed as her students continued to learn all subjects taught in English. Our students participated in learning Portuguese taught by the methodology Eloisa Lima describes in this book. It was active, engaging and fun for young students! The enthusiasm and dedication demonstrated by the DICE teachers was commendable. In their short time in Orlando these teachers taught basic Portuguese to our English speakers and prepared them for an end of program performance presented to our students alongside the DICE students.

The cultural exchanges also included a beautiful display of artifacts from Brazil for all students to visit and learn from. Also the DICE teachers prepared a sampling of typical foods and sweets for the teachers and staff of the host school.

The DICE students' immersion into our classrooms provided them with a rich educational environment in which to continue to use the English taught in their school in Brazil. Eloisa Lima and the DICE Program are to be congratulated for a unique learning experience for both Portuguese speakers and English speakers.

Margarita Vega
Retired Principal
Orange County Public School

PART I

AUTHOR'S NOTE

I started to develop this methodology close to educator Lauro de Oliveira Lima and by the occasion I had the opportunity to work in several pre-schools with children ranging from 1 to 12 years old. Beforehand, I wish to state that this experiment was not limited only to the English language. THIS METHODOLOGICAL APPROACH IS APPLICABLE TO THE TEACHING OF ANY LANGUAGE or other study objectives, resulting in this manual which contains a wide spectrum of pedagogic material which is also open and subject to the inclusion of new discoveries. Therefore, we are going to communicate in English so as to reach a greater number of educators.

In view of the complexity of the Piagetian Theory, we must make it clear that it seems rather difficult to cover the whole universe of possible activities and content of this book. As the pedagogic idea is so creative and wide, it would have a limiting effect to reduce it to a simple "didactic book". What is being presented, however, constitutes a set of pedagogic activities and exercises that may be reduced or enlarged, according to the particular conditions under which any work is being carried out.

Rio de Janeiro, July 26, 2018
Eloisa de Oliveira Lima
The Author

B CONSTRUCTIVISM: USAGE AND PERSPECTIVES IN EDUCATION

- The search for methodology
- The starting point
- The growth and strengthening of the idea
- Dealing with a new linguistic code and developing the intelligence of the child

Before we even begin to understand the content of this methodological work, it is necessary to explain how and why another path, one that differed from the old and well known "Pedagogy of Contents", so rigid, so traditional, so strong throughout the world even today, was taken.

A phrase directed at me by Professor Lauro de Oliveira Lima – who will be referred to later on – was the PROBLEM-SITUATION of all research that makes the teaching of a second language at a very early age, feasible. The phrase was:

I was eighteen years old at that time and had had the opportunity to participate in the establishment of a kindergarten and Elementary School named "A Chave do Tamanho". At this point, work never before undertaken in the field of Education began, under the authorization of Jean Piaget. This consisted of applying the Psychogenetic Theory to Education known as the C.E.E.J.P. (Centro Experimental e Educacional Jean Piaget), responsible for this pedagogic experiment. Under the guidance of Professor Lauro de Oliveira Lima, a group aimed at the study of the Jean Piaget's interactive theory in quest of an active, participative methodology that, above all, would develop the intelligence

" Find out how to make these children speak English

of the child. As far as I was concerned, all this was still in the embryonic and very complex stage, because I had just started my high school studies. I kept asking myself how to employ a revolutionary methodology in the teaching of a second language to pre and post literate children, without providing ready-made replies or conditioning them to boring exercises, but at the same time arousing a liking for the object of study and more importantly:

A critical and systematic observation of work developed in the classes at the schools helped me to grasp what each level of mental development could understand of their world, how language was developed in a child from the earliest stages.

When I was 23 years old, I started to work with Junior school levels (1st and 2nd segments) at Canarinhos Camaiore Secondary and High School in Rio de Janeiro. This school was known for its rigid discipline and accelerated presentation of material content to students. The creation of didactic materials based on the knowledge of the groups (2nd segment of the 1st grade) was not permitted. We had to use materials written by well-known authors (the teacher would not dare to create anything, only reproduce what already existed). The work carried out in group's dynamics was "noisy" and consequently, forbidden.

After having worked for several years in a school using traditional teaching methods, I came to the conclusion that expository teaching was boring and disagreeable, as well as silent and lacking in questioning on the part of students. On the other hand, it was easy to see how children produced very much more with Dynamic Group proposals: there was more happiness and tonus when they were able to vibrate when participating in a game, for example.

I concentrated on mounting basic visual material by hand, starting from an organization of the world, so as to arrive at a universe that was closer to that of children. The objective was to allow the child to learn meaning/significance without the need to translate. (This will be dealt with in more detail in the specific chapter).

At this time, many schools, especially pre-schools, began to experiment this psychopedagogical methodology, offering their students a differential in the foreign language study process.

In 1986, I was invited to work in a kindergarten school which followed the Montessorian methodology. While there, I had the firm conviction of testing everything: the material created on the basis of Piagetian work, the methodology, students' reaction, parents' reaction to the new method of teaching their children. Once again I was able to definitely establish the efficacy of the method: the children showed a great deal of interest and actively participated in the activities proposed.

Having perceived the absence of any work developed in regard to the English language for children at pre-school age, I felt the need to preserve and perpetuate this methodology with loyalty and faithfulness, including the way students absorbed new sounds and new linguistic codes.

To the teaching profession which over the years has been depreciated and eroded, thus, many times, leading teachers to lack creativity I offer this support to those who still hope for transformation in teaching.

To the children who rebel against the sameness of repetition, there was the intention of affording more satisfaction in the study of a language.

THE EPISTEMOLOGIST AND THE PEDAGOGUE: JEAN PIAGET AND LAURO DE OLIVEIRA LIMA

Jean Piaget was born on August 9th, 1896 in Neuchatel, Switzerland, a small university town. While still very young he had already written his first article based on his observations of sparrows. He later began to study mollusks as a voluntary assistant to the local museum of history, which was of immense interest to him in the field of Biology. After receiving his Honorary Doctorate in 1918, Jean Piaget concentrated his professional interest in Psychology. He worked in the Binet laboratory, where he became interested in children's thought patterns, by means of clinical methods. He was, undeniably, one of the greatest scientists in human behavior research that the world has known.

He was an epistemologist. Epistemology is a branch of philosophy concerned with the theory of knowledge, from which he developed what is known as Psychogenetic. This theory advanced along a path that was opposite to the theory which stated that intelligence is determined by hereditary influences alone. Observing and questioning children, he was able to establish that intelligence is developed gradually, going through distinct phases and links until reaching its highest degree: abstract operations.

According to him, the greatest psychologist-epistemologist in the world at present, intelligence is not innate (its pre-conditions are innate). According to him, the development of intelligence is equal to the development process of an embryo or the transformation of a seed into a plant: it is a construction where each succeeding structure embodies and compounds previous structures (each structure becomes a sub-component of the next structure).

Piaget states intelligence develops philogenetically (evolution of human beings) as much as ontogenetically (the development of each child). The development of each child continues until it reaches the level of the group in which the child forms part. Therefore, the stimulus a child receives from the cradle will determine the level of intelligence that will be developed.

It is worthwhile stressing that Jean Piaget restricted himself to the study and explanation of human development without being concerned with pedagogy. At that time there was no "Piagetian – pedagogic method". However, he did have an idea as to the importance of his theory in relation to Pedagogy: "I am convinced that my work can be of service to Education, provided that it goes beyond a theory of learning and does not lose sight of other methods of acquiring knowledge."(Jean Piaget).

In 1921, Edouard Claparède, director of the Jean Jacques Rousseau Institute in Geneva, invited Piaget to occupy the post of Director of Studies at that Institute, where he remained for many years. He divided his activities among other institutes such as UNESCO, as Director of the International Bureau of Education; the Center of Genetic Epistemology, as founder; apart from his function as Senior professor in Psychology at Sorbonne Institution. Piaget was highly decorated, honored and respected throughout the world. Among the first of his great works is **"Le Language et la Pensée chez L'Enfant"** (1923) [The Language and Thoughts of Children], which conclusively proves, through his scientific method that the development of language acquisition respects a cognitive development criterion.

Lauro de Oliveira de Lima born in Ceará, Brazil in 1921, after having studied Junior High School in his home city, continued his studies at the Jundiaí Seminar, São Paulo, Brazil, from 1935 to 1940.

He became a secondary school teacher, giving classes

in Latin, French, Geography and Portuguese. In 1945, by means of a Public Selective Exam, he was appointed to the position of Federal Inspector of Education, a post he held for twenty years, ten of which as Sectional Inspector for the Ministry of Education and Culture in Ceará Brazil. He graduated in Law in 1949 and, two years later, in Philosophy.

He then decided to leave the sphere of private teaching to establish a secondary school, creating a Teachers' College and a primary school where he started the reformation of pedagogic methods. He started the practice of teaching and learning through a group dynamic, proposing the psychogenetic method based on Jean Piaget's theories of development. He was awarded the Chair at the Institute of Education in Ceará, where he promoted the reformation of the Teachers' College teaching methods. He was a member of the State Education Council, a governmental assessor participating in all educational movements in the State between 1957 and 1963.

He was a professor of Experimental Psychology at the Catholic Faculty of Philosophy and Fortaleza Faculty of Social Psychology. On behalf of "CADES" (a governmental teachers' training department) he offered development classes to high school teachers. In 63/64 he was director of High School Education for the Ministry of Education and Culture in Brasília (Brazil's capital), where he completed the first global planning for this sector of the Ministry. With the Military Dictatorship of 1964, his political rights were canceled, and he was only reintegrated in his chairs of professorship in round about 1990.

As an educational scientist, after a protracted study of the Piagetian Theory, he decided to create a pedagogic method that was entirely based on the Swiss psychologist's Theory. This theory is based on the development of the child's intelligence; that is to say:

EACH AND EVERY LEARNING PROPOSAL MADE TO A CHILD SHOULD CONSIDER THE MENTAL LEVEL OF THAT CHILD AT THE TIME THE LEARNING PROCESS IS CONDUCTED.

Based on this contention, a PROBLEM-SITUATION should be created to accompany, as a basis (an assimilation scheme) for the previously prepared application.

There is no teaching: means are provided for the child to discover and reach the proposed objective.

Having dealt with all school system phases, he created, in Rio de Janeiro, "Centro Experimental e Educacional Jean Piaget" (The Jean Piaget Educational and Experimental Center), authorized by Jean Piaget.

THE TEACHER DOES NOT TEACH: THE STUDENT IS HELPED TO LEARN.

LAURO DE OLIVEIRA LIMA

THE PIAGETIAN TEACHER

A change in the view of education

To educate through intelligence means leading a child, from birth, and constant stimulation, to invent, to discover, to acquire and construct, using his or her own initiative and the use of the unexpected to reach the highest degree of autonomy.

For this reason the Piagetian teacher follows a path that is removed from that of memorization, conditioning, routine habits, pre made results based on models, without being concerned with the process employed by the student in working with the situation.

To be a Piagetian teacher means: challenge, criticism, a great deal of determination to create argument, attempts, tips and hints, options, research sources, the unusual, the new, originality and never supplying the answer.

In this way:

THE TEACHER DOES NOT TEACH: THE STUDENT IS HELPED TO LEARN. (L.O.L.)

The concern of this teacher should be directed at the performance of intelligence that is: which thought processes a student employs in rationalization, and not the result in itself. Excessive help given by an adult inhibits the student's creativity, many times hindering the opportunity.

The teacher, however, must promote a difference of opinions among the students; solicit creative ways out or solutions that are different from existing customary ones.

THE TEACHER HAS NOT RIGHT TO INDOCTRINATE, NOR EXPRESS OPINIONS. (L.O.L.)

The only thing that does not "count" is to refuse to carry out a proposed previously analyzed task when it is adequate to the mental level of the student. In the pedagogic activity, "all is fair", the student is free to carry out a task in a spontaneous and creative manner, subject to guidance, thereby respecting the basic rules of psycho-socio-cultural development.

Our affection for the students should be intimately linked to the objective of our problem-situation. The teacher's tonus on approaching the objective is the thermometer of interest the group displays in relation to the object being studied. Therefore, we must love the object of our study and remember that:

ONE CAN ONLY LOVE WHAT IS KNOWN. (L.O.L.)

Consequently, on presenting a theme with assurance to a group of students, we are challenging and stimulating them more and more to interact with the object of studies in process.

"Every intelligent act has a level of dedication that corresponds to the degree of interest that the activity provokes and the whole state of dedication is demonstrated by a determined operative level (intelligence), that is: THERE IS NO INTELLIGENCE WITHOUT EFFECTIVENESS AND THE OPPOSITE IS EQUALLY TRUE. We work alongside a powerful challenge of "love and firmness".

Intelligence is employed to confront PROBLEM-SITUATIONS and there can only be problem if there is questioning. If this is not the case, no doubts arise: either it is obvious (too easy) or it is a mystery (there is no solution) and therefore, too difficult. Consequently, developing intelligence is based on the creation of the correct problem-situation, one that is adequate to the level of mental development of each student.

Once the PROBLEM-SITUATION has been solved by the group, it becomes the teacher's task to discuss the results – directing the conscience towards a generalization of the idea. This should occur jointly, never discarding the relationship of the children with the group and always in the language in the study.

We now reach an extremely delicate question of the didactic performance of this new educational view – LINKING (sequence and graduation of problem-situations). Continue challenging the group, without there being a lowering of interest, paying heed to the structuring of the next situation after the one solved previously by the child: this is the sequential constructivism formulated by the Piagetian Theory of Development of the Intelligence.

The game centers on an effective artifice whereby a PROBLEM-SITUATION is proposed to the group.

A Piagetian teacher should adopt the stance of proposing

A GAME IS TO A CHILD LIKE WORK IS TO AN ADULT. (L.O.L.)

healthy competition between groups. We will dwell on this very useful proposal further on in this treatise.

> **EVERYTHING TAUGHT TO A CHILD INHIBITS DISCOVERY AND INVENTION ON THE PART OF THAT CHILD. (JEAN PIAGET)**

From the psychopedagogical point of view, we can schematize fundamental characteristics, considering the average ages of each stage of development while never forgetting to provide a good margin of flexibility among them. Each child has his or her own optimum moment of reaching mental maturation.

- *Why "suffer" to learn?*

Many people think that to learn a foreign language it is necessary to experience a tiring process of sentence or vocabulary repetition in order to really dominate the language. We can make a quick comparison with physical exercises designed to develop muscles. Doing these exercises over and over again increases the biceps. If this process were to be transferred to the teaching of a language, it would be to think that the more times a sentence is repeated the faster the communication of that structure will happen. Thus, examples such as these summarize the aberration in respect to both cases, both in the learning of a second language and the building of muscles. It would be a serious mistake to state that physique can only be strengthened by means of specific therapy, thereby removing the cogitation of a game of sport.

Thus, in learning a second language, one should not think that artificially repeating, memorizing would make things easier in a real communication situation, whether it be oral or written. It would be very much more effective to create, at all times, an unusual situation in real life, either "make-believe" (through games), which challenge creativity and causes a wide and natural means of communication.

Consequently, the different methodologies based on mere repetition, conditioned reflexes, are tiring, give rise to boredom and are not efficient, because they deal with language in a formal way, resulting in the loss of stimulus and subjecting the creative individual to suffering.

COMMENTS ON EXISTING METHODS EMPLOYED IN THE TEACHING OF A FOREIGN LANGUAGE

J.C. Richards in *The Secret Life of Methods* proposes two types of classification for existing methods of teaching a foreign language: based on the formulation of a "syllabus", that is, on a programmed content to be explored and, instructional methods, based on a theory of teaching/learning a Language.

The methodology presently being examined falls into the second category. Basing the Theory of Psychogenetic Development together with the pedagogic model created by Lauro de Oliveira Lima, a method in which the English language is presented to children between the ages of one (or since they start speaking) to 13 years old, respecting the mental levels proposed by Jean Piaget, is established.

However, our work and research objective, the Language, is in itself specific. According to Richards and Rodgers in the article "The Nature of approaches and methods in language teaching", for a method which may be deemed efficient, it is necessary to determine the view of the Language adopted by such method. Our next topic is to explain this point of methodology.

For didactic purposes, the three views of the nature of Language present in any method may be summarized as follows:

Structural:
The Language is seen as structurally organized system to express meaning. The emphasis of this concept of language is centered, however, on form.

Functional:
The Language exists to express functions (desires, greetings,

displeasure, etc...). Thus, the focus is no longer on form in the daily use of the idiom. It is noted that the same form can express different functions, in the same way that the same function can embrace a number of functions.

Interactional:
Language is said to be "a vehicle for the realization of interpersonal relations and for the performance of social transactions between individuals (…) a method for the creation and maintenance of social relations". (Richards, 1986)

The "Syllabus"- programmed content – of this methodology only contains the two first views, as we feel that the target-students (children aged 12/13 years old), have not – as yet completely developed discursive strategies in their own language. Anecdotes, ambiguities, metaphors, etc, are not totally understood in their mother language and, as we see it, these are necessary for performance in a "Syllabus" based on an interactional view.

Therefore, it becomes necessary to present the child, at the outset, with the existence of another linguistic code in order to refer to the world surrounding that child. This other linguistic code not disassociated from the context in which it operates, acquires, however, with its own functional value. The children are resented with the possibilities of being able to express themselves in different functional forms, with a choice based on the type of interpersonal relationship, formal/informal register, hierarchical difference between interlocutors, etc. Together with the functional character of enunciation, focus is primarily given to fundamental grammatical categories found in the context and production of enunciation always employed in the act of communication. Consequently, syntax and semantic aspects are presented simultaneously to the students. Oral production comes from the exploration of the sentence and it is amplified by small texts at the beginning of reading and writing.

In the second chapter dealing with APPROACHES AND METHODS IN LANGUAGE TEACHING, Richards subdivides the method into three inter linked stages: "Approach", the theoretical framework upon which the method is based; "Design" (a course plan), where the objectives, the contents are organized, the learners activities and the roles of the teacher, the students and the material to be used, are defined and, finally, "Procedure", classroom practice. In each of the points focused, Richards establishes criteria for the examination of teaching/learning methods in relation to a second/foreign language. We will now follow the stages, aiming at an analysis of the elements and sub elements that make up this Methodology.

GENERAL OBJECTIVES AND METHOD SPECIFICS:

As our method is based on a theory of knowledge, it has as its general objective the placing of the child in his or her social group. Thus, on presenting a new possibility of expression, we are also contributing to the child's educational process and their capacity to respect the other. In the belief that any teaching/learning method should consider the "school" institution in our society as being a contributor towards the formation of individuals as a whole, there is a social role to be performed. When it comes to the method in question, dynamic groups contribute towards the achievement of such objectives.

In regard to the English language, our aim is to develop the ability to understand right from the beginning, because we believe that this is the first step before speaking. According to Krashen, the type of input received by the student should be "understandable" through actions, gestures, mimicry, interesting (or attractive), taking into consideration the mental level; "not grammatically sequenced, in sufficient quantity – and experienced in low anxiety contests" – by means of games, music, etc. See "Procedure" in the detailed description of methodology (Richards, 1986).

In relation to the roles played by the students and the teachers, it can be said, as we deal with children and accept them as being heteronymous, we believe that all pedagogic activity should be controlled by the teacher, who determines the tasks to be carried out by the class and promotes interaction between the students. The way in which we handle our "Procedure", as well as the "Syllabus", will be dealt with in the pertinent chapter.

THE STAGES OF MENTAL DEVELOPMENT: A DESCRIPTION OF MENTAL LEVELS ACCORDING TO THE PSYCHOGENETIC THEORY

• *Behavioral characteristics in each level of mental development*
• *Why, when, and how the study of a second language should be initiated in an early age*

Jean Piaget classified the evolution of thought in levels or stages, discovering that in a child, until he/she reaches the abstract operative level (the moment at which he/she can come to his/her own conclusions), he/she goes through the same process which the whole of the History of Humanity did until coming to the point it has nowadays (The Stone Age, The Age of Fire...up to the present High Technological age).

According to Piaget, a child is born with everything to learn, bringing with him/her only hereditary inheritances (genetics) and the first reflexes (suction and grasp). All with the same possibilities, except if something slows down development.

There is no "Genesis", the maximum intelligence found in a human being is hypothetical-deductive intelligence or probabilistic or combinatory mathematical logic (INCR Algebraic Group).

From birth to two or three years of age, Jean Piaget classifies child thinking as sensorial motor (STAGE I – Sensory Motor). The child's major expression is through body actions.

From three to four, five years of age children go through a symbolic phase (STAGE II – Symbolic), when native language reaches its peak.

From five to six, seven or even eight years old, they are classified in the pre-operatory phase called the Intuitive

Period (STAGE III) and Concrete Operatory (STAGE IV). Finally, at the age of twelve, the child should be starting the Abstract Operational Period (STAGE V). Between thirteen and eighteen, the adolescent should be effective in abstract intelligence, unless something has interfered with or obstructed mental development.

During the teenage period, the intelligence continues maturing into "Hypothetical Deductive Thought". We must direct our attention to certain extremely important aspects before starting a study of these mental levels, which are:

a) We are talking about children who are absolutely normal from the genetic and psychological point of view;
b) The ages mentioned here are not rigidly fixed, varying from child to child, environment to which they belong, stimulus received, and even the school at which they study. The individual may be highly developed at every step of intelligence, because this is the capacity required to deal with variables aimed at solving a problem;
c) The levels are not seen separately; each one embodies and compounds the previous one. Therefore, a symbolic child, for example, continues to be a sensory-motor.
d) We only mention the most important characteristics of each mental level, suggesting that the teacher makes further studies of each level in order to gain a better understanding of the development of the children with whom he or she is working.

It is very important to understand that these mental levels are linked and one upper level depends on the previous ones. In case a child loses the chances to exercise and live with others (human beings need to deal with other children on their level and with younger and older ones to develop their own thinking process).

STAGE I — SENSORY MOTOR PERIOD – FROM BIRTH TO ABOUT 3 YEARS OLD

The first intelligence model that is developed and which is the basis of "practical" behavior. The construction and the development of six stages take place during this period. According to Jean Piaget there are important issues as main points during the growth of the human being.

1) Reflex Exercises;
2) Primary habits: suckling, for example;
3) Coordination of sight and grasp: the baby grasps and handles everything that he or she sees around and is satisfied with any action (rattle) or object (feeding bottle), in this way forming a secondary "circular reaction"(the baby is gratified by the prolonging of the spectacle);
4) The discovery of new situations (coordination of secondary reactions);
5) The discovery of new means (tertiary circular reaction);
6) Interaction of schemes and "deduction" of new ones.

It is during this period that "Object Permanency" is established, that is, the world and its objects continue to exist, even though they may not be present within the child's field of vision. This conservation of the permanent object occurs over the sensory-motor period and ends after a period of twenty-four months.

This period is the most fertile in transformation and raises a child to a level that is superior to that of a monkey, making active practice possible (automatic or creative).

It is during this period that the first sound indications appear. The crying stage continues to about the second month of life. The emission of sound similar to the sound of a vowel continues to about the fifth month. The syllabic babble "ma-ma-ma-ma", or echolalia: the repetition of syllables or words for the mere pleasure of emitting sounds, with no concern as to whom they are being addressed or even heard, neither bothering to pronounce words that have a meaning, continues for about a year after the child's birth. It has been noticed that children who are born deaf reach the babbling stage, but soon after the sixth month of life it ends, thereby confirming the process of language acquisition during this period, defining the most elementary stages of maturing organisms. At the end of this period a rough outline of the mental image begins and, at the same time, language and drawing begins to show themselves – it is what Piaget calls SEMIOTIC FUNCTION.

We arrive, then, at the correct moment to begin the work of foreign language acquisition: the action level.

When we say "sit down here", we must immediately imitate the action, and make the child repeat it: in the same manner that a child constructs his/her mother language: ACTION until IMITATION. Hear / Understand / Imitate with ACTION.

We conclude, at this point, the general explanations about one of the most important aspects relating to the acquisition of a language, no matter which, and that of a second language. The subject, one that has caused so much argument in field of phonoaudiology, refers to how the human phonological system is engaged. As with everything that is undergoing a process of formation, there is flexibility and plasticity, subject to molding. With the passing of time the individual grows, reducing the possibilities of development and manipulation of his or her intelligence. This also happens with language; however, the more a child has been stimulated within each level it is found, the greater the possibilities will be for the development of his/her intelligence.

In regard to the phonoaudiological system, the more we "practice" new phonetic models with a child, the greater will be his/her capacity to pronounce sounds he/she hears. We must allow the child to hear the words pronounced correctly and be careful not to repeat what the child has reproduced at his/her level, by pronouncing the words in an infantile manner When a child says, for example, "bled" instead of "bread", it is because that child has not yet phonologically reached the final stage of its phonological apparatus. It is still trying to do so. The child thinks that the reproduction was faithful to what was heard by him/her. Whatever a child hears there is an effort on the part of the child and an attempt by means of trial and error, and the adult is wrong in thinking that the word "bled" will help the child to understand: on the contrary, it hinders the imitation of the correct pronunciation, which comes from the result of correct sound production.

We must, therefore, construct language by manipulating words without prejudice, but always working at the mental level of the child in question. For a sensory motor child having a small vocabulary we still cannot form sentences without demonstrating them by way of action and making them imitate the action in a practical way.

> When we say: "Let's jump over this rope", we must ACT and REPEAT. Repeat to each one when acting and do not translate! Action, movement is the crux of understanding by SENSORY- MOTOR children.

STAGE II — SYMBOLIC PERIOD – FROM 3 TO 4/5 YEARS OLD

We consider a child to be symbolic when he/she makes the objects surrounding him/her malleable. For example, a chair serves as a car, a car which he/she will drive, go to school, be a parent. This is the start of what Piaget calls the "Symbol Game" or game of fiction, which is, without doubt, the peak of infantile games.

In this phase, the child's language is budding; he/she repeats everything he/she hears, he/she is always imitating sounds (onomatopoeia). Language is based on symbolic thought (animals have no access to this phase). We now enter an EXCELLENT moment in time for the learning of a foreign language. I say EXCELLENT because this is the phase in which a child shows total interest in STORIES and, by means of this activity, we can work the structures of language more easily and intensely, apart from there being a vast vocabulary without "censure" on the part of the child caused by a social fear of committing errors of speech and criticism.

The child is not yet concerned with the details of the words employed. The important thing for the child at this point is to be delighted with the sensations that the story transmits. The child begins to relate to the characters and lives the story as if it were his/her own life.

> Consequently, during this period of mental development, we must transform each activity into a story, so that a goal can be reached by means of that story. At this level, the child lives the story as if it were "true".

The symbolic period is very rich and should be intensely explored by teachers for children. It is important to remember how diverting and flexible symbolic thought is, since this is the instrument we will be using with children. The symbolic child is highly egocentric, still centered around his/her own point of view, talks to him/herself and makes up stories with his/her toys, reproduces situations based on his/her day to day existence and is capable of transforming the world, symbolically, in order to satisfy a momentary need. As far as children are concerned, objects have life; when they hurt themselves on a table, they are capable of hitting the table as if the table was something alive. The child is magic, contradictory, not yet LOGICAL, but PRE-LOGICAL.

During this period, "deferred imitation" as in the sensory-motor, would not occur. This imitation represents the start of acting in thought (MENTAL IMAGE). The more we stimulate games of "make believe", the more we promote the child's cognitive development and emotional equilibrium.

Symbolic children appear to talk to each other; however, if we pay attention, we notice that the phrases do not coordinate between them; they all speak at the same time. Piaget classifies this level of language as Collective Monologue; it is the most social of egocentric varieties among children as it combines the pleasure of speech before others and attracts or appears to attract their interest in relation to the child's action and his/her own thoughts.

At the age of five/six years old, still symbolic but now able to very well distinguish between fantasy and reality, the language evolves to what Piaget calls Adapted Information – the child wants to be heard, wants to communicate something to the interlocutor but, however, is not capable of maintaining a conversation. The child changes the theme the moment he/she hears a word that arouses his/her interest; he/she adapts his/her reply to other phrases;

Child A: "I went to the beach; there was sun"
Child B: "The sun is there on the mountain making it warm".

We must take full advantage of this level to explore stories, dramatizations, music, and drawings. The children are now capable of reproducing simple structural sentences and generalize on other objects (Ex: open the door, open the can), as well as repeat everything heard, because there is "maximum exercise" of the language.

STAGE III — INTUITIVE PERIOD – APPROXIMATELY 6/7 SEVEN YEARS OLD

Now, that symbolic child is no longer the same. The child can now differentiate between fantasy and reality and, when alluding to fantasy, he/she uses "let's make believe that". It is a transitory stage between pre-operatory and operatory level.

The intuitive child shows a great deal of interest in the causes of phenomena and this is why he/she is always asking questions – it is the famous "why" age. Whenever a child is asked how he/she knows a certain thing, he/she replies that he/she always knew, nobody taught it to them; they become artificial (everything was done by man).

A child is capable of organizing collections and sets. He/she now accepts games that have rules. Moral is rigid, no concessions are made, "eye for an eye, tooth for a tooth".

Verbal expression is important; the child is no longer satisfied with general understanding, he/she wants to understand every word that makes up a phrasal structure. The time has arrived for detailing, descriptions of paintings, the retelling of stories; he/she reveals a curiosity about the written word.

The language level now reaches that of ADAPTED INFORMATION, which is still intense during this period, the DIALOGUE – the child maintains a "conversation", without, however, being able to argue different points of view in order to arrive to a common consensus. Dialogue continues for quite a time, until he/she reaches the next level.

STAGE IV — CONCRETE OPERATORY PERIOD – FROM ABOUT 7 TO ABOUT 11 YEARS OLD

The child at this stage is concluding numerical conservation related to substance and weight. He/she is able to see totality, and is no longer centered on only one point of view as he/she was when symbolic intuitive. He/she can now organize the world in a coherent manner; his/her thoughts are now more flexible.

He/she can now make use of SIGNS (words) and for this reason the time has arrived to start teaching how to write (see details of the teaching of writing – later chapter).

The child now accepts dramatizations as if in a theater play. Verbal language becomes more important and now they converse at length with friends. As thoughts are now concrete, the child loves constructions, detailed assembly kits, guessing games, puzzles, charades, and we can make good use of these resources. A child is able to play games having complex rules.

The language level remains at the dialogue stage for a long time to come. Only when the child is about eleven, twelve years old he/she is able to exercise discussion, it is when the adolescent is able to argue a theme having different points of view and try to come to a conclusion.

STAGE V — ABSTRACT OPERATORY – 11/12 YEARS OLD ONWARDS

At this stage, the child is free of the concrete phase. He/she is entirely removed from the object. Now thoughts are hypothetical-deductive, they have their own opinion and are able to argue and discuss for hours on end. Socially, the child lives in a group and is able to establish relationships of reciprocity and cooperation.

It is important to remember that the passing from one stage to another does not necessarily mean getting old. There are many adults, chronologically speaking, who have not reached total development of thought in the abstract operations level. Intellectual challenge and experience amplifying each stage is fundamental for a "qualitative jump" from one level to another. The base of the pyramid is at the SENSORY – MOTOR level.

HOW TO DEVELOP THE LANGUAGE OF CHILDREN

• *The Semiotic function*

Before going into details, we must draw attention to some extremely important statements in order to have a better understanding of the method.

IT SHOULD BE MADE CLEAR THAT THOUGHT (INTELLIGENCE) IS NOT A PRODUCT OF REPRESENTATION, BUT COMBINATIONS THAT MENTAL ACTIVITY CREATES WITH THESE PRODUCTS. (L.O.L.)

Language takes time to appear in the development of a child, it only appears between the first and second year of life.

A minimum of "logic of action" is needed, logic which is fundamental in dealing with language in itself.

Language is intimately linked to objects: while a child is not about to perceive the absence of objects; he/she is not capable of forming the image of an object in the mind.

According to Piaget, intelligence is an **attribute of action**, opposing the proposition that it is derived solely from perception. The intelligent act is a combination of a preventive and procedural acts.

Preventive activity is constituted by perception, language, representation, imitation, experience and comprehension. This activity corresponds to the SEMIOTIC FUNCTION.

It is a "sine quae non" condition for something to be represented. Any "meaning", then, becomes passive through a "meaningful" existence.

Mesa, Table, etc. (The object is the meaning)

Mesa, Table, etc.

(the name given to the object becomes meaningful)

This representation occurs in language, mental image, symbol gesture, imitation, drawing and symbolic game.

The procedural activity refers to movements, shifting of positions, classifications, thoughts, serializing, etc.

The highest degree of SEMIOTIC FUNCTION development is that of language. This is a socialized semiotic product, codified and conventional. It is socialized as it is shared by all speakers; it is codified because it obeys series of specifications (of that idiom) and conventional because it follows paradigms and criteria that identify that language in relation to others. It requires logic, as every language has its own inherent logic apart from structures, peculiar schemes and organization. Thus, for a child to make use of the language – that spoken and written by his/her social group – the child has to organize the logic of actions. Piaget distinguishes the prior moment of language itself, calling it pre-language. This moment certainly marks the start of representation; it is characterized by imitation of an action on the part of the child, or the way a non-codified individual symbol is used.

Specialized language is no longer referred to in certain scientific subjects, it is denominated as post-language.

This semiotic function appears near the end of the SENSORY-MOTOR stage and that is when the symbolic period begins. The last phase of the sensory-motor stage is characterized by the outset of the semiotic function.

We are, therefore, at this moment, before the open doors of an ideal receptive scheme for language, supplied with safe support for the introduction of other languages.

At this stage, the language begins to bloom accompanied by action, like a kind of onomatopoeia, followed by the use of the word.

For the psychopedagogical process, it is important to clarify immediately that the possibility of learning a language is carried out by conditioning, through mere conditioned reflexes. We are born able to breathe spontaneously. However, in order to speak and articulate language, one needs models.

Imitation is the first indication of the SEMIOTIC FUNCTION. Imitation evolves until the model is no longer necessary. This is what is called Deferred Imitation, which is not only representation, thought, but makes the act a general symbol, one which the child responds to immediately. Now, contact with others permits the establishment of communication.

Drawing, in its turn, has a real representation in a more rudimentary form than language, as it is less employed socially.

Language is incorporated as a social product by mere imitation of sound, which means one should pay attention to see if the child knows what he/she is producing in language.

We should explain at this point the importance of language in the global development of intelligence, aiming at an understanding of the structural proposal of the current method.

The acquisition of language in a constructivist way represents an activity and, thus, develops intelligence. On working with a linguistic structure, one operates with logic in particular, making it possible to increase significance tenfold, amplifying and giving agility to thought schemes.

We therefore can conclude that the SEMIOTIC FUNCTION contains a number of thought representation forms, based on the permanence of the object, organizing thought and beginning to act at about eighteen months after the birth of the child.

DEVELOPMENT OF READING – LITERACY: A KNOW-HOW

There is an exact moment within the vast process called THE TEACHING OF READING AND WRITING where a high content of the practical work is dedicated to the achievement of perfection. Children feel anxious about reading/writing because they know their parents can read and write. So much so, that there are schools in which content of material to be explored with children is fragmented at this time.

- *Is this moment important?*
- *Can the moment of learning how to read and write arrive suddenly?*
- *Should we disassociate READING from WRITING?*
- *How can the child's life experience so far contribute to READING?*
- *Can those who know how to read, know how to write?*

There is much controversy over a moment that is nothing more than know-how, a work tool. Let's attempt to understand the meaning of READING within the process of knowledge. READING is the recognition of the world in which we live. It is by living, holding, feeling, seeing, smelling, tasting, hearing, etc, that the individual carries out reading, which is, in one sentence THE READING OF EXPERIENCE. The richer this experience is, the more fundamental and better will be the cognitive development.

Consequently, what we have to understand by THE TEACHING OF READING AND WRITING is a process that can only be fully carried out if the child holds, hears, creates, experiments and combines, constructing, in this way, the words of thought and practicing, exhaustively, speech. The fact that the child is in a position to express experiences in phrases serves the scheme of assimilation whereby the child obtains the possibility of dealing with significance and meanings. In order for this to occur, it is of the utmost importance that concrete operatory thought has already been established, naturally widening the need to know how to read. This code reading then forms part of the individual in the same way that "holding" was fundamental in reading the world whilst still in the embryo stage-sensory-motor. The literate individual never again discards this instrument at any time during his/her cognitive activity. That which was, until then, only available in audio-visual form has now been added to by a visual/written form.

We, at this point open parenthesis to establish a distinction between READ and WRITE. Roughly speaking, one action is not understood without the other. It is necessary, at this point, to clarify why we must separate these two moments. They are two distinct processes from the cognitive point of view. On the one hand we have READING, where the subject is merely receptive. On the other hand, at the time of writing, the subject is emitting, producing. Writing appears after reading; in the same way that speaking occurs after action. We are able to read about a subject, understand it, but without having the ability to write about it.

Joining letters, vowels, the vocalic "families", spelling words; all techniques that stimulate the achievement of literacy do not invalidate the time a subject needs to mature the reading process. It is of the utmost importance that the subject is apt to receive this know-how as a fundamental part needed for a "safe journey", widening his/her field of action and his/her possibilities of getting to know the world that surrounds him/her.

Without doubt, at this moment, learning to read flows rapidly without having to ignore the whole or to live other activities and pedagogic experiences so necessary for mental development.

This disassociation is clearly observed when a second language is presented in the form of the written word: the children read on the basis of assimilation with ease. The same does not happen simultaneously with writing. There is an appreciable register of absence when using the assimilation scheme for writing. This scheme furnished by Gestalt (the law of good form, proximity, similarity) as proposed by the current methodology in reading. As soon as the student has the scheme of reading in mind, writing becomes available as a new tool of communication.

Returning to the generic question of reading (called the global process of literacy), we reiterate that our concern when working with children on another linguistic code is to avoid an "overlapping" of knowledge construction stages: hear, understand, act, speak, read and write. The option for writing should be accepted at the right moment; should this not occur it becomes a useless tool and, therefore, artificial, inadequate and inopportune. There is a lot to be said before writing. Writing is only a part of what Jean Piaget defines as the SEMIOTIC FUNCTION, which is a thought organizing function that embraces not only reading and writing but a mental image, language, drawing, imitation, as well.

Being able to read should mean being ready for what is needed. The child needs to have a repertoire of world experiences to actually start reading.

Now let us turn to a specific case dealt with in this book: the acquisition of a second language. We will attempt to elucidate fundamental questions with which both educators and parents struggle when facing native language with a second language.

- *What is the right moment for a written second language to be introduced to a child?*
- *Is it prejudicial for a child to be taught how to read and write in two languages simultaneously?*
- *Can confusion between the two languages occur when a child is being taught?*

Well, we will begin by distinguishing children according to their experience. A bilingual child (exposed to two languages at the same density, quality and time) will be in a practical position to distinguish the right moment and speak adequately in each of the languages. This child has the same possibilities in either language, capable of reading both simultaneously, without confusing them.

Occasional mistakes made in reading or in writing are perfectly compatible with the reality being experienced by this child, who is still moving towards generalization. As soon as reading has been generalized and activated, the better and more understandable will the reading of one or the other language become. The dominium of this know-how now falls to effective practice.

In regard to the case of non-bilingual those who only have one language in preponderance and the other language being acquired on a lesser scale (this student is less exposed to a second language than a native), we must respect language knowledge process and its mental development. The more we make a child speak before the start of the writing phase, the better. We once again must remember that reading should be confined to reading material that is within the child's knowledge gained through experience (oral); should this not be the case, the child should be literate in his/her own language, taking the pronunciation of this language sounds as a reference, reading a word in English (in this case) as if it were pronounced in their mother tongue. An artificial situation without precedence is then created, causing serious damage to the gradual maturation process expected in this second language. We then have, as a result of these maladjustments, a child having to face a large number of difficulties because of a lack of an assimilation scheme, or very painful pronunciation vices, consequently causing a loss of stimulus for the learning of a second language, which in many instances cause the child to give up and reject the language being studied.

The most relevant causes of this imbalance arise from

either the fact that it is not known what to do with a child who does not know how to write yet or -worse -how to amuse and satisfy the student already literate. This makes that student abstain from writing in a second language, which he/she speaks little in a classroom. These are the two nerve points of this discussion.

In the face of this evidence, we resort to the hypothesis that the earlier a child begins acquiring other languages, the earlier that child will be "ready" for writing.

This problem does not end here. We remember cases of students who started their studies of a second language only after they had become literate in their native language. This, in many instances, comes about through the unawareness of parents who, very often are lay people in relation to the subject, deem it necessary to know how to write in order to know how to speak a language, even including language courses, committing the error of starting the teaching of a second language through writing.

Consequently, we see a large mass of students suffering the illness of language study by "indigestion", "forced" to study, without the least pleasure, because they have been robbed of assimilation schemes.

It is up to the teacher to promote a real methodological metamorphosis in didactics with students starting the study of languages. With firmness and sensitivity, the teacher should keep the class attractive, and at the same time creative enough to stimulate oral activity through interaction among students to the maximum, without the need for writing as a solution to the proposed PROBLEM-SITUATIONS.

With no doubt, the reading of these languages, worked at the right moment, will be rapid and efficient, even more so because the know-how of reading, already acquired by the native, undertakes to help in the task of introducing the student to reading in a second language.

# *VERY IMPORTANT EXPLANATORY VOCABULARY RELATED TO PIAGETIAN NOTIONS EMPLOYED IN PHSYCHOPEDAGO GIC METHODOLOGY*

Having to dedicate a separate chapter to Piagetian notions is due to the fact certain "popular" expressions defining them in an entirely different way are used, although it is worth remembering that they are always very well explained when under study, making it possible to understand them within the context of his theory.

One of the expressions most subject to misunderstand is that of ASSIMILATION, which popularly means that the person who assimilated the lesson understood the "material presented", thereby increasing that person's knowledge. According to Jean Piaget, "assimilation" is an act that does not modify the subject; it is only feedback, leaving the subject in an unaltered state (like watching television or listening to the radio). We should not confuse learning with the old learning process, derived from conditioned reflexes, where after an exhaustive process of repetition and memorization, learning is presumed to have taken place.

Jean Piaget calls ACCOMMODATION (which does not mean that the subject is appeased), the moment of "gain", modifying the way of thinking and acting. In order for accommodation to occur the subject is required to know how to deal with the PROBLEM – SITUATION which has an un-settling effect, making a resort to an ASSIMILATION SCHEME (something known) necessary which will furnish means to solve the PROBLEM – SITUATION proposed. As soon as this PROBLEM-SITUATION has been solved (according to the mental level), it means that the subject has performed an intelligent act – the subject "learnt".

IMITATION is an effort of verbal or mental motor manipulation which produces the object in order to understand it. IMITATION is the initial step towards the development of intelligence. Nothing "new" is learnt. The known, the old, is assimilated, which furnishes the means of action leading to ACCOMMODATION, (the new), thus the importance of assimilation. The subject is able to assimilate without accommodating, but can never accommodate without assimilating. ACCOMMODATION is combinatory, a complex process which demands assimilation first. Creativity is based on previously manipulated models, furnishing weapons for invention / creation.

Jean Piaget calls the whole process an adaptation and balance between ASSIMILATION and ACCOMMODATION. They are the successive accommodations made by the subject that constitutes the development of INTELLIGENCE.

TO EDUCATE CAUSES IMBALANCE

Educators should not lose any opportunities for a practical approach related to this theory and we should remember that a game is one of the widest forms of stimulating new combinations. As to EMOTIONAL DEVELOPMENT, an issue widely dealt with by psychologists, we can say that this represents the spine of the psychogenetic theory and, in terms of the psychopedagogical approach of this theory; EMOTION acquires dimensions compatible to that of intelligence.

EMOTION is the propelling charge that engages intelligence. EMOTION, therefore, is the TONUS of behavior, the degree of interest shown by the subject for the activity, it is the strategy employed by the subject in approaching the object.

Exemplifying the relationship between teacher-student: the student's interest in the object is proportional to the TONUS of the teacher to present a PROBLEM – SITUATION. If the latter strongly dominates the object of study, there will certainly be a complete emotional charge, with a lot of TONUS, a great deal of affection directed at the presentation of the object / proposal of the PROBLEM – SITUATION. This affection is constantly maintained, rising or falling according to how the proposal fits the mental level of development.

We, once again, take the opportunity of putting the theory into practice, referring to the fact that everything is based on ACTION. EMOTION for one's own body and/or manipulation based on an experiment: exploration of the physical qualities of the object, "discovery": logical-mathematical experiment, organization of the field of action relative to the object; "invention". The grammar of a language is the organization of the object's possibilities.

Pierre Greco understood the Genetic Epistemology of Jean Piaget as theory of "opening", with possibilities of achieving new "possibles". This opening establishes the axel of constructivism, successively entering into a state of what-is-to-be. Thus, the constructivist method works on this result, generating an infinite number of PROBLEM – SITUATION possibilities, from which, provided there are adequate assimilation schemes, will generate ACCOMMODATIONS and, consequently, learning, therefore, an intelligent act.

Opening corresponds to invention or the so called creativity. In this way, the constructivist theory consists of requiring the greatest possible quantity of variations from the subject, "do it another way". Language, at a creative moment constructing entirely new phrases, new situations, is a classic example of opening.

We take the opportunity at this point to criticize behavioral conditioning in the teaching of languages, which through conditioned reflexes, proposes the fixation of a pre-defined model for each supposed situation. Once we know that there is not one moment equal to another, each instant being original, containing something different, we can see the defective character of learning by means of conditioned reflexes.

Therefore, the degree of creativity results from the capacity to combine new forms, to achieve an infinite number of varied possibilities.

SEQUENTIAL CONSTRUCTIVISM is Piagetian structuralism:

THERE IS NO STRUCTURE WITHOUT GENESIS, NOR GENESIS WITHOUT STRUCTURE. (JEAN PIAGET)

MENTAL IMAGE is yet another very significant expression within the Piagetian theory of cognitive process. This image occurs through the object's interior, point for point, imitation. For a better understanding of a MENTAL IMAGE, we take as an example the affirmation that a child first perceives the diffcrence between a complete circumference and one in which a piece is missing before he/she can tell the difference between a circle and a square – the child firstly perceives the image of a continuous line of dots.

The SEMIOTIC FUNCTION is a process that embraces the MENTAL IMAGE, although it is constituted only after the appearance of this occurs. The SEMIOTIC FUNCTION begins with imitative manipulation of the object and continues with interior or deferred imitation, in the absence of an object. It is the SEMIOTIC FUNCTION that permits thought and reaches its peak with language.

"To learn how to speak" is to couple mental image with codified conventional sounds, interiorized sounds that develop into drawings and writing, both codified (signs).

In regard to our object under study, language, we should mention that its development does not determine the parallel development of operations, despite the fact that the reciprocal is true.

Observe the deaf and dumb who develop intellectually, although alternative means of communication are used.

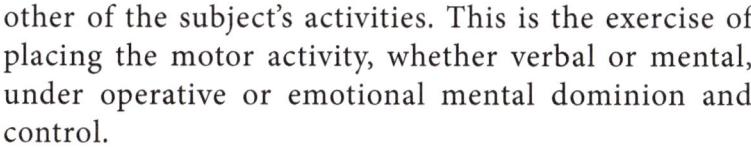

According to Piaget, Becoming Aware is another of the subject's activities. This is the exercise of placing the motor activity, whether verbal or mental, under operative or emotional mental dominion and control.

Returning to practice, as an example, we would ask a student how a certain result for a supposed problem-situation was arrived at, being careful, however, not to induce him/her into determined answer.

Teacher,
Be creative.
Do what you have done before but, do it differently.
Discover or invent a new problem-situation for your students.

We could go on at length by displaying words employed in this theory, transforming this material into just another reading of Piaget; this would be of no value.

We leave this chapter open to inclusions that will no doubt occur as greater involvement with this psychopedagogical practice takes place. Our entire proposal merits reading of not only that which is contained herein, but during the coming to the professional maturity of the teacher.

PART II

HOW TO PLAN AN ENGLISH CLASS IN TERMS OF THE PIAGETIAN APPROACH

- Ascertain the average of the group. From this point, satisfy yourself as to which mental development level the group is classified, according to the theory proposed by Jean Piaget.

The teacher will certainly know or should find out whether the students forming this group maintain or have maintained some contact with the language to be taught. This group should then be evaluated as to their proficiency in this language.

- Once in possession of the data mentioned above, the teacher will then be able to determine the following aspects:
- *How an Activity should be presented to the Group of Student.*

Each mental level should have a different proposal, that is, to sensory-motor children, an ACTION activity should be proposed. To "symbolic" children, stories, fantasy, dramatizations. To intuitive children, who no longer accept fantasy, there is a need for guessing games, strong challenges, games, construction, theater, plays. Operative children should be exposed to more focused activities, stories without pictures, descriptions, games, construction in groups.

- *Duration of Proposed Activities*

Firstly, check the total number of minutes available for the class and, based on the principal objective, distribute and dose the activities dividing the maximum time of concentration for each of the levels of development.

- **Sensory-motor:** *the activities should not last more than seven minutes; on average, five minutes.*
- **Symbolic:** *the activities can continue for about ten minutes*
- **Intuitive:** *activities can last up to fifteen minutes.*
- **Operative:** *activities can last up to twenty minutes.*

It is important to remember that these "times" of duration are not rigid and are intimately linked to the interest the group shows in the activity proposed. Should the activity be too easy for the group, it may be done or completed in less time than was originally planned. It is important that the teacher in each period of "time" be aware of the exact moment that interest either awakens or declines in regard to the activity undertaken by the group. The teacher should end this activity before students lose total interest in it. As soon as the "optimum moment" is reached (the moment at which there is the greatest interest in the activity), its termination should be proposed.

- *Physical space used*

The teacher should endeavor to totally use the physical space available to him (classroom and other areas as well): use the floor for the formation of groups (in a circle all the students will be seen and see each other), vary its placement, exploring prepositions and organization, separating fixed pairs. The teacher should also pay attention to alternating activities carried out at a table and on the floor. The teacher should make the students move! This is very important, mainly at sensor-motor level. To assure group productivity, it is fundamental that the students do not become exhausted.

- *Material to be used during each activity*

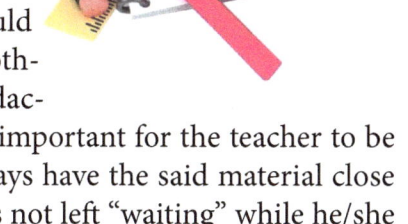

The teacher should have previously separated the material and make sure that each student receives an equal distribution of it. Should there be insufficient material, the activity should then be substituted by another. In regard to teacher didactic material, it is extremely important for the teacher to be very well prepared and always have the said material close at hand, so that the group is not left "waiting" while he/she organizes the lesson.

- *Assimilation scheme*

On proposing an activity, the teacher should have previously explored a simple activity, one that should also constitute a simpler problem-situation that will serve as a pre-requisite for the execution of a more complex activity.

THERE IS NO GENESIS WITHOUT STRUCTURE, OR STRUCTURE WITHOUT GENESIS. (JEAN PIAGET)

One cannot create from nothing.

ACTIVITY PROPOSED – ASSIMILATION SCHEME PREVIOUSLY EXPLORED

Draw a story in two parts – Draw a story
Cut out in a curved line – Use scissors cut out in a straight line
Explore parts of the paper – Explore all the paper

- *Complexifying*

The teacher must always make sure that the activity is complexified for those students who are more apt and faster, thereby achieving the objective well within the time provided for such activity. By giving more complex orders to these students, the teacher will, in this way, avoid a loss of interest in the activity.

Example:

ACTIVITY – COMPLEXIFYING
Cut out in a curved line – Color in the curved strips
Make a boat in this sea (Symbolic) – Draw on half the paper – Turn the paper over and draw on the other half

- *Generalization*

All work content must be generalized. To generalize means that there has been learning; for this to occur, all possible shapes must be explored so as to exhaust the possibilities within the level of the group concerned.

Example:

All the chairs available in the classroom should be recognized by the child, that is to say, the different models, and types of chairs should be explored by the teacher in the language being taught. The child should recognize these objects as "chair".

- *Direct and inverse operation*

Whenever working with a notion, the teacher should be ready to explore direct and inverse operation, such as, for example, open/close, go/come, in/out, on/under, etc.

- *Revision*

Many times we do not achieve the generalization of a concept with certain students. Thus, every class should be planned to contain one or more activities from the previous units, always widening and complexifying the use of vocabulary, to make generalizations possible.

Games are very adequate activities for the achievement of this objective, and research on this point can be planned.

It is important to remember, however, that every activity should be creative, challenging and must stimulate intelligence.

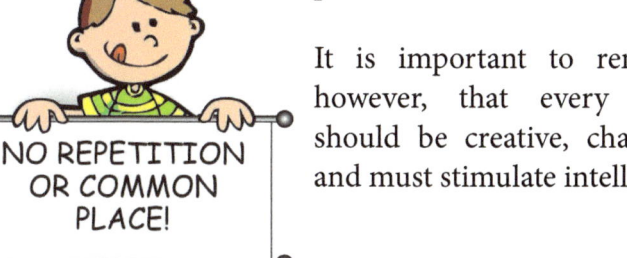

- *Working material for teacher and student*

- PEDAGOGIC MATERIAL:
  1) **Consumable**
  2) **Didactic**

A well planned class using this methodology should function like a "school"(the one where they have regular classes), thus transferring to the English language all the activities and routines normally worked with the children, taking into consideration, of course, the stage of development the children possess. It follows, therefore, that different types of material should be especially classified as: consumable and didactic. Before arriving at such specifications, we have observed that the English language should be the most important material used in this methodology, as any language is only spoken with fluency if the structures are practiced.

Not a single opportunity should be lost when teaching a foreign language. All daily actions, social rules, organization (discipline), tidying up and cleaning of the classroom after the completion of activities, congratulations, admonishments, compliments, and so on, should be worked in the language in focus.

Avoiding the use of native language is a constant task in this methodology and the teacher must not be afraid to use the language he/she is teaching, although care must be taken when using such a language at the mental level of those being taught. Sensory-motor and symbolic children, for example, do not understand conjunctions and the use of more refined expressions, not even in their own language. This then, requires that short, objective and easily demonstrable sentences be used when talking to them.

1) CONSUMABLE MATERIAL

Sheets of papers, cardboard in various colors, off white paper, scissors, pencils, crayons, glue, colored pencils, chalk, eraser, colored marking pens, plasticine. If necessary, a diary and a drawing pad may be included.

This material may be used collectively, and its distribution being the responsibility of the teacher at the commencement of each activity. The students, may, however, have their own material. The first option allows the teacher to explore all this material as well as to organize and also make sure the activities will take place. It's important that all students have the material needed so that they can have the experience necessary for that class.

As well as materials, we also suggest some TECHNIQUES which are really valuable when teaching young learners. They are:

- POP-UPS: To cut and fold paper in a way that it pops up from a card.
- DECOUPAGE: To cut out pictures to decorate boxes, notebooks, picture frames, chest. Then varnish them with clear glue so they can shine.
- PAINTING WITH BLEACH: Wet cotton swab in bleach to draw on kite paper/tissue paper.
- ORIGAMI
- FINGER PAINTING: To draw on different kinds of paper using finger and finger paint.
- COLORED GLUE ON CELLOPHANE PAPER
- PASTING USING DIFFERENT MATERIALS: To paste using beans, rice, noodles, pieces of paper, wool, etc.

- TRANSFIX: To transfix something by putting a paper over it and scrabbling a crayon over it.
- DRAWING WITH WET CHALK: To wet pieces of chalk in water and draw on different kinds of paper.
- DRAWING ON SANDPAPER USING CRAYON OR CHALK
- PLAY-DOH
- DRAWING WITH DROPS OF MELTED CRAYON – To draw using crayon melted on the light of a candle.
- STENCIL: To draw, color or paint using a shape.
- MAKING THINGS OUT OF SCRAP

All the activities above are an extra occupation with the language while contextualizing the order given.

2) DIDACTIC MATERIAL

2.1) GENERAL

2.1.1) STORYBOOKS

The teacher may also arrange his own library. The books must be appropriate to the units being explored; access to the school library or even a temporary library should also be contemplated. In this case, each student, from period to period, would bring a book, (preferably in English, which would widen the use of the book for the groups who have already read it) previously selected by the teacher and then returned after having been used.

2.1.2) Games

Greater attention to this material will be given at a later stage, as it represents the core of the practicing of the whole pedagogic proposal. All indoor games (memory, puzzles, games played on a board, etc.) or in teams that aid in practicing the language, will serve as didactic material. (See chapter "Suggested Activities that accompany the Methodology").

2.1.3) REAL OBJECTS

All kinds of real objects in plastic or toys (miniatures) will be of immense value. In the same way that a library is formed, a collection of objects classified according to some criteria, should also be made. These objects will serve in storytelling, games, mimic, etc.

2.2) SPECIFIC

This material constitutes and constructs the entire reading of the word process according to Gestalt (exhaustively worked through meaning). In English, the separation of syllables is avoided so as to prevent the boredom of having to recognize the letters phonetically, which is not necessary because we are dealing with a second language and the child should already know how to read and write in its native language. This in itself will furnish an assimilation scheme sufficient to transfer the word (Gestalt) to phrasal construction. There is a lot to be done orally before going on to reading the language.

Card board in different colors by language categories should be provided by the teacher for reading games.

2.2.1) FLASH CARDS

We propose a system that moves from reality-based input (cards with images only), reaching a certain moment when real world objects are presented together with words, and ending when only words are used. This system aims at removing the child from the extra linguistic realm by gradually putting him/her in touch with linguistic one.

The First Cards:

Photographs or clear drawings of nouns. These must be as realistic as possible and follow some criteria of classification. These cards may be called "First Cards". They are used for reading games, correspondence with real objects, substitution drills, etc. They represent very important material as far as the teacher is concerned.

(1) Refer to the chapter on the teaching of **Reading and Writing**

Second Cards:

Just like the first cards, they present explored vocabulary, but now containing the meaning (word) that corresponds to the object. They should only be handled by the students who have already dealt with the first cards and who, however, know how to pronounce the sign presented, correctly. This will prevent the child from being influenced by the written word, wrong pronunciation caused by using the mother tongue as a phonetic reference.

Third Cards:

These only carry the words themselves. They are grouped according to the grammatical function they normally exercise within the language structures and must be presented in different colors.

- ACTIONS (verbs)
- MODIFIERS (adjectives)
- ADVERBS
- NAMES/THINGS (nouns)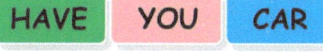
- DEMONSTRATIVE PRONOUNS
- INTERROGATIVE PRONOUNS
- NUMERALS
- CONJUNCTIONS
- PREPOSITIONS

They are written front and back as follows:

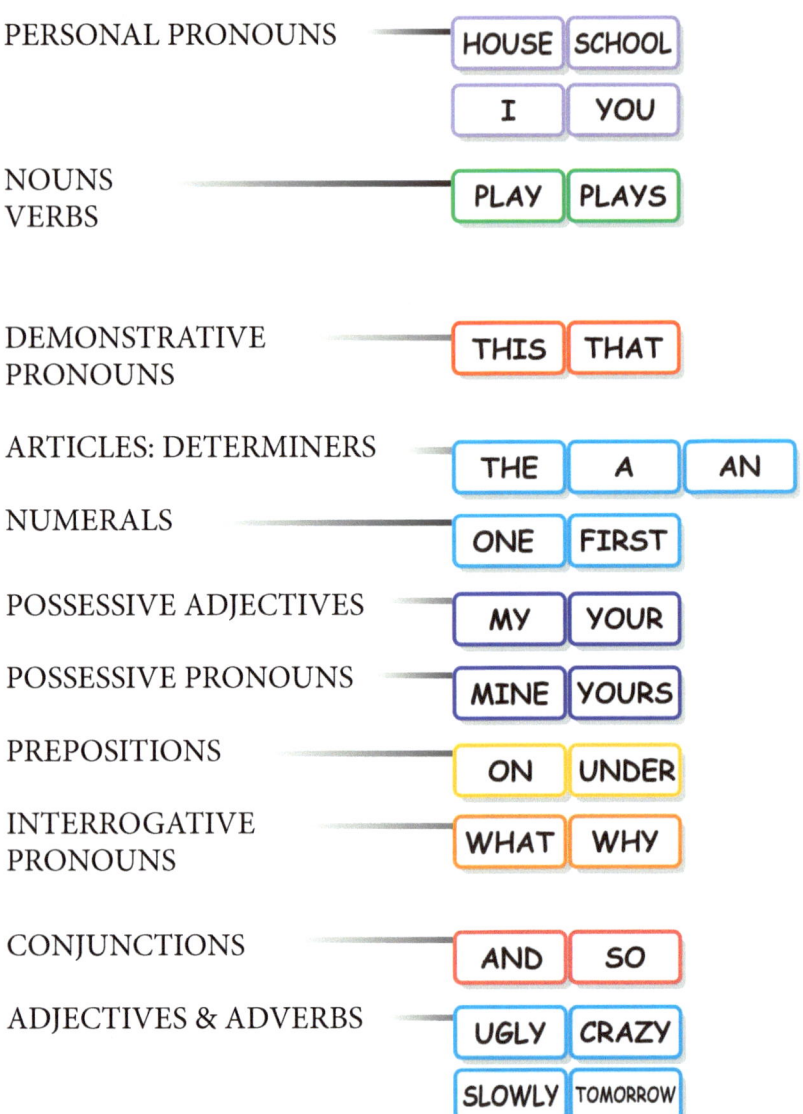

They must be introduced over what the students have already generalized orally. From this moment we define two objectives in our planning (1) that which operates exclusively in oral terms which is already used in complex phrasal structures and more specific vocabulary, and (2)

that which refers to the field of reading, which follows the structures that are generalized by a student, i.e., the simplest one. Therefore, the reading problem-situation is the "becoming aware" of the written code related to what the student already dominates orally.

We deal with the process of literacy using this methodology in a special chapter.

2.2.2) CDS AND DVDS

The teacher should select songs sung by other people (preferably native voices) to explore music with their students. These songs should be anything from kindergarten songs, folk songs to popular songs, and explored according to the mental development level of the group.

The teacher should always be ready to record the students singing or record oral activities in the classroom. It is very important for the children to hear other voices and their own voices played back on the recorder. Apart from helping them become aware by comparing pronunciation, this activity is very attractive to children. Symbolic children live the magic of this technology and the more operative children feel less uneasy about fluency at this level.

2.2.3) SCRAP

All and every kind of material should be used by the teacher to carry out different activities which can also be explored in English.

Example:
Cloth, lids, boxes, pieces of wood, nails, needles, different textures of paper, Styrofoam, paint, etc. The teacher should be interested in any kind of material that will allow the children to explore the names of things in English that make up the world surrounding them while stimulating creativity.

2.2.4) Magazines

The teacher should have magazines available for cutting out pictures, making paste-ups, mounting photographs and words in English (for levels that are working on writing).

2.2.5) Dictionaries

A dictionary should always be included as a part of didactic material. If a teacher should not know the name of an object in English, a dictionary should be consulted together with the children, thereby teaching them how to handle one. This includes children who already know how to read.

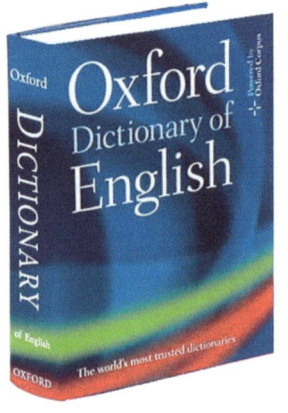

There are a number of illustrated dictionaries on the market. The teacher should analyze what is the most appropriate for the level being taught. Preference should be given to monolingual editions; photo dictionaries are excellent because they remove the student from their mother language.

Every need, whether it be a thing, an action, quality should be dealt with in the language under study. The less interference there is from the native language, the faster the foreign language will be internalized.

B THE CLASSIFICATION OF THE UNIVERSE

- *How to organize the vocabulary universe in the study of a foreign language*

This Methodology functions on the basis of carefully selected units drawn from the world that surrounds the children – family, school, food, etc.

We start with generalities and progress towards particularities, because the greater the quantity of specifics, the more the theme should be understood. It is important to remember that these units should be dosed according to the level of mental development found in each group. Ideas that a child is still not able to understand should not be proposed. For example: family relationships form a network, and third party relationships are not yet generalized by small children. Many times a word is used, but they do not construct the notion. Ex. "She is my father's sister-in-law". If we ask what the relationship between the child and sister-in-law is, the child does not understand this kind of family connection.

Below you can find a suggested sequence of units, distribute.The term Levels here refers to the age and the mental development stage of the student. Thus, a two-year-old that is in an early sensory-motor stage should start in

Units	Levels												
	1	2	3	4	5	6	7	8	9	10	11	12	13
Family	5	5	5	5	5	5	5	5	5	5	5	5	5
School	4	4	4	4	4	4	4	4	4	4	4	4	4
...	...	...	...	...	...	...	...	...	...	...	...	...	...
Animals	5	5	5	5	5	5	5	5	5	5	5	5	5
Nature	4	4	4	4	4	4	4	4	4	4	4	4	4

Level 2, study **FAMILY, SCHOOL**, etc and then do it all over again in Level 3, and 4 etc until he/she reaches Level 13. The difference is the complexity of **FAMILY**-related structures from Level 1 to 13.

The number inside the squares represents the number of classes that should be used for each unit. Spending 4 to 5 classes dealing with one topic is a relatively big amount of time. The course planner must have in mind that less relevant topics demand fewer classes.

The units are merely a suggestion, but we believe starting with **FAMILY** and **SCHOOL** makes a lot of sense because these are two very important realities in students' lives. Also, the sequence must be established having in mind some logical reasoning. For instance, if you are teaching **NATURE**, probably you are going to need to make students aware of an array of vocabulary related to animals. Then, it just seems more reasonable to teach **ANIMALS** first.

We also suggest some "extra" units like **MOTHER'S DAY, EASTER, XMAS, CHILDREN'S DAY**, that is, celebrations which are part of the student's cultural reality. They make students more aware of the importance of these dates in their country and also offer a refreshing break from the everyday units. Units like **THANKSGIVING DAY** or **HALLOWEEN** are advisable as well, since they are cultural phenomena attached to the language students are learning.

Classification by unit can obey a number of criteria; the teacher will define beforehand how the students are to be introduced to the world. Several schools organize their syllabuses in contents as well. If the teacher is aware of the contents his/her students are learning at school, he/she can profit from this and use them in his/her English class.

Once having defined the theme of the lesson, the parts of speech should follow the same theme. Consequently, actions, qualities, adverbs, prepositions, etc., must be concerned directly with the theme to be dealt with.

Example:
Theme: FOOD

The appropriate actions to be dealt with must be: eat, drink, like; adjectives; nice, bitter, cold, hot; adverbs; at the table, in the restaurant, at the free-market, in order to develop the theme with less or more density according to the level of mental development and degree of advancement in the study of the language being taught.

Once again, the need for fluency in the language is stressed and there should be no concern with the use of structures covering all tenses of the verb. Make use of the language to cover the requirements that arise at the moment and do not be concerned as to whether the children will or will not understand the reasons why. Do not forget that a demonstration of what is being said, in ACTION, is absolutely necessary. Our speech must be accompanied by action and expression the feeling must be intense and constant acting the "TRANSLATION" of what we say.

We have a suggested list of units and they are as follows:

And here you can find some ideas on what to approach in each unit:

*   **Family:** Greetings, relationship, different places of living (house, building, and apartment), downtown, suburbs, neighborhood, directions, parts of the house (rooms), and parts of the body, daily commands, nationality, and main language related to family.

*   **School:** School, classroom, objects used, permanent furniture, school building, schoolmates, people that work at school, things we make/do at school, directions, greetings, subjects, schedule, vacation, snack, tests, field trip.

***Food:** Everything you eat. Fruits, Drinks & Kitchen Things are dealt with separately, but they should be worked on next to Food in general, market, supermarket, restaurant, meals, snack bar, cost of living (money), salt, sweet, dairy products, frozen food, fast food, transgenic food.

***Fruit:** Fruit salad, grocery, fresh, artificial, smoothies, shakes

***Drink:** Hot, cold, fresh, shakes, soft drink (sodas), artificial, sparkling water, juices, milk, water.

***Kitchen things:** Everything we use to prepare the food, to eat, to set the table, cutlery, electronic appliances.

***Nature:** Things of nature, natural phenomena, geographic features, weather, seasons, date (date, month, year), summer saving time, countries and nationalities.

***Animals:** Domestic, pet, wild, zoo, forest, farm, insect, flying animals, sea animals, pre-historical, extinct animals, feather, skin, fish, bones, food they eat, habitat, research, seasons and weather, vertebrate, invertebrate.

***Clothes:** Kinds of clothes, weather, shops, stores, department stores, fashion show, beautiful/ugly things, when/where to wear what, seasons, places, accessories, old-fashioned, date, patterns, classic, fashion, updated, old, ridiculous, ugly, awful.

***Cleaning Things:** Hard cleaning, personal cleaning, stuff used for cleaning, different soaps, different appliances, dirty, clean, maid, service, hard work, house cleaning, dusty, laundry, ironing, brushing, support staff, custodian, and janitor.

***Transportation:** Different means of transportation, how do you go to a certain place? Why? Where do you go by? Old/new, who drives a _____? Traffic, travelling, traffic signs, city, roads, freeway, city map, guide, traffic lights, directions.

***Travel:** Vacation, short trip, journey, camping, different ways of travelling, passport, English speaking countries, globe, world, tour, hotel, farm, fun, entertainment, pleasure, professional, check in/out, city tour, sightseeing, field trip, adventure.

***Communication:** Means of communication, talking, chatting, writing, reading, interviewing, discussing, phoning (calling), recording, singing, listening, video games, letters, post cards, movies, watching TV, video, DVD, computer, musical instruments, e-mail, remote control, zapping.

***Sports, Games & Toys:** Competition games, playing, enjoying, entertainment, Olympic games, sports students like/prefer, matches, saloon and field games, children (nice/boring), playground, winter/summer sports, toys, wheel sports, computerized games, electronic games, virtual, arcade, attractions, theme parks.

***Professions:** People's different kind of work activities and occupations. What do you want to be?; What are your parents' professions?; Where do the people work?; rich, poor, salary, occupation, novelties, retirement, benefits, allowance, paycheck, pay stub, hire x fire.

***Celebrations:** Anniversaries, birthdays, Christmas, Halloween, Easter time, children's day, mother's day, father's day, Thanksgiving day, Independence day, Valentine's day, others.

***General Things:** Everything that does not include any other category described above.

Below you can find a list of nouns for 1st and 2nd Cards by unit:
(To be used during all classes as vocabulary support. These flashcards should be designed under the same style for all suggested 12 units)

Unit 1: Family
1-aunt 2-baby 3-bathroom 4-bedroom 5-double/single bedroom 6-boy 7-building 8-family 9-father 10-garage 11-girl 12-grandfather 13-grandmother 14-house 15-kitchen 16-living room

Unit 2: School
1-adhesive tape 2-agenda 3-blackboard 4-books 5-chair 6-chalk 7-classroom 8-crayons 9-desk 10-dictionary 11-door 12-eraser 13-flag 14-floor 15-folder 16-glue 17-paint 18-knapsack 19-map 20-marker 21-notebook 22-notepad 23-pair of compasses 24-pair of scissors 25-paper 26-paper clip 27-pen 28-pencil 29-pencil case 30-pins 31-photocopier 32-ruler 33-school 34-stapler 35-student 36-table 37-teacher 38-wastepaper basket 39-window

Unit 3: Fruits
1-apple 2-avocado 3-banana 4-cherry 5-grapes 6-honeydew 7-kiwi 8-lemon 9-orange 10-papaya 11-peach 12-pear 13-pineapple 14-plum 15-strawberry 16-watermelon

Unit 4: Food
1-barbecue 2-beet 3-birthday cake 4-black beans 5-bread 6-brocolli 7-cabbage 8-cake 9-carrot 10-cauliflower 11-cheese 12-chicken 13-chocolate 14-cookie 15-corn on the cob

16-crackers 17-eggplant 18-eggs 19-french fries 20-fried egg 21-garlic 22-green beans 23-ham 24-hamburger 25-hot dog 26-ice cream 27-jam 28-jello 29-ketchup 30-lettuce 31-lollypop 32-mayonnaise 33-muffins 34-mushrooms 35-mustard 36-onions 37-pancake 38-pepper 39-pie 40-pizza 41-popcorn 42-popsicle 43-potatoes 44-pudding 45-pumpkin 46-salad 47-sandwich 48-soup 49-spaghetti 50-steak 51-sundae 52-tomato 53-turnips

Unit 5: Drinks

1-beer 2-coffee 3-coke 4-hot chocolate 5-milk 6-milkshake 7-orange juice 8-tea 9-water 10-wine

Unit 6: Kitchen Things

1-blender 2-bowl 3-coffeemaker 4-cup & saucer 5-fork 6-glass 7-jar 8-knife 9-microwave oven 10-mixer 11-mug 12-pan 13-plate 14-refrigerator 15-spoon 16-stove

Unit 7: Animals

1-alligator 2-ant 3-wolf 4-bear 5-bee 6-bird 7-butterfly 8-cage 9-camel 10-cat 11-chick 12-rooster 13-cockroach 14-cow 15-crab 16-cricket 17-dog 18-dog house 19-duck 20-elephant 21-fish 22-fly 23-frog 24-giraffe 25-goose 26-grasshopper 27-hen 28-horse 29-kangaroo 30-ladybug 31-lamb 32-lion 33-monkey 34-mosquito 35-mouse 36-octopus 37-owl 38-parrot 39-peacock 40-pig 41-rabbit 42-rhinoceros 43-sea horse 44-shark 45-shrimp 46-snake 47-squirrel 48-tiger 49-turkey 50-turtle 51-zebra 52-zoo

Unit 8: Nature

1-beach 2-cloud 3-flowers 4-forest 5-garden 6-leaf 7-moon 8-mountain 9-rain 10-rainbow 11-river 12-rock 13-roses 14-snow 15-star 16-stone 17-sun 18-thunder 19-tree 20-flower pot 21-wind

Unit 9: Clothes
1-bathing suit 2-belt 3-bikini 4-boot 5-cap 6-dress 7-glasses 8-glove 9-hat 10-jacket 11-jeans 12-necklace 13-tie 14-pants 15-pullover 16-purse 17-raincoat 18-ring 19-shirt 20-shoes 21-short 22-skirt 23-socks 24-tennis shoes 25-T-shirt 26-umbrella 27-watch

Unit 10: Cleaning Things
1-broom 2-bucket 3-comb 4-cotton swab 5-dental floss 6-dustpan 7-hairbrush 8-lipstick 9-mirror 10-perfume 11-shampoo 12-soap 13-sponge 14-tissue 15-toothbrush 16-toothpaste 17-towel 18-vacuum cleaner

Unit 11: Transportation
1-airplane 2-balloon 3-bicycle 4-boat 5-bus 6-car 7-garage 8-helicopter 9-motorcycle 10-rocket 11-ship 12-submarine 13-subway/metro 14-terminal 15-train 16-truck

Unit 12: Communication
1-audio CD 2-cassette tape 3-CD player 4-CD rom 5-comics 6-computer 7-DVD player 8-DVD 9-laptop 10-digital camera 11-drum 12-e-mail 13-guitar 14-keyboard 15-magazine 16-mobile phone 17-mail box 18-memory stick 19-microphone 20-tablet 21-newspaper 22-piano 23-wi-fi 24-stamp 25-tape recorder 26-telephone 27-television 28-video 29-video tape 30-earphone

Unit 13: Sports, Games & Toys
1-ball 2-balloon 3-basketball 4-bowling 5-car 6-cards 7-checkers 8- chess 9-doll 10-game cube 11-kite 12-ping pong 13-puppet 14-puzzle 15-roller skating 16-seesaw 17-skateboard 18-slide 19-slot machine 20-soccer 21-surfboard 22-swimmer 23-swimming pool 24-Teddy bear 25-tennis racket 26-video game 27-volleyball

Unit 14: Professions
1-ambulance 2-artist 3-astronaut 4-band-aid 5-clown 6-cook 7-dancer 8-dentist 9-doctor 10-driver 11-engineer 12-firefighter 13-firetruck 14-hammer 15-magician 16-medicine 17-lawyer 18-nurse 19-painter 20-patrol car 21-police officer 22-postman 23-screw 24-screw driver 25-secretary 26-shot 27-singer 28-thermometer 29-waiter 30-workman

Unit 15: General Things
1-ashtray 2-bed 3-bill 4-box 5-bulb 6-calendar 7-candle 8-chain 9-chest 10-cigarette 11-city 12-clock 13-coin 14-fire 15-flashlight 16-hanger 17-iron 18-keys 19-ladder 20-lamp 21-lighter 22-matches 23-money 24-picture 25-sofa 26-wallet

Unit 16: Travel
1-bag 2-binoculars 3-camera 4-credit card 5-globe 6-hotel 7-lamp 8-GPS 9-passport 10-suitcase 11-tent 12-tourist 13-trailer

Unit 17: Celebrations
1-bat 2-candle 3-Christmas ball 4-Christmas bell 5-candy can 6-Christmas Tree 7-Easter egg 8-Easter rabbit 9-Frankstein 10-ghost 11-haunted house 12-presents 13-pumpkin 14-reindeer 15-Santa Claus 16-skull 17-sleigh 18-snowman 19-stocking 20-Thanksgiving 21-witch 22-wreath

And here you can find a list of words for 3rd
Cards by part of speech:
(The indicated colors for the cards are not rigid. They are used front and verse under the same part of speech)

PREPOSITIONS
COLOR: YELLOW
about/at; across/between; across/through; after/to; before/after; beside/behind; for/by; from/to; in/on; in front of/next; in front of/behind; inside/outside; of/off; on/off; on/under; out/in; up/down

POSSESSIVE PRONOUNS & ADJECTIVE PRONOUNS
COLOR: WHITE
my/your; your/their; his/her; its/our; your/their; it/his; her/my; mine/yours; yours/his; hers/its; ours/yours; ours/theirs; yours/his; his/hers

DEMONSTRATIVE PRONOUNS
COLOR: ORANGE
this/that
these/those

ARTICLES & NUMERALS
COLOR: BLUE
one/first; two/second; three/third; four/fourth; five/fifth; six/sixth; seven/seventh; eight/eighth; nine/ninth; ten/tenth; a/an*; a/the*; an/the*
*half card

ADVERBS & ADJECTIVES
COLOR: SALMON
intelligent/stupid; interesting/boring; large/extra large; light/dark; light/heavy; more/less; more/than; much/many; neat/messy; never/always; never/today; no/yes; often/rarely; old/new; old/young; orange/brown; pretty/ugly; purple/green; rich/poor; sad/happy; short/long; small/large; smart/dumb; soft/dumb; sometimes/hard; tall/short; thick/thin; today/yesterday; tomorrow/today; too much/a little; well/poorly; wet/dry; white/blue; yellow/purple; black/white; wealthy/poor; always/

never; than/much; few/a few; a lot of/not many; a lot of/too much; always/often; beautiful/ugly; big/little; clean/dirty; delicious/famous; easy/difficult; green/blue; best/worst; better/worse; careless/careful; most/least; some/any; here/there; beast/beauty; -ier/-er; favorite/sweet; ever/never; every/always; everyday/now; expensive/cheap; fast/slow; generally; frequently; good/bad; high/low; hot/cold; -er/-iest*; -est/est*
*half card

PERSONAL PRONOUNS
COLOR: WHITE (half card)
I/you; you/they; he/she; it/we; they/we; we/you; it/she; you/I; he/you

CONJUCTIONS
COLOR: BROWN
but/and; or/because; than/so; but/and; or/because; than/so; but/or

INTERROGATIVE PRONOUNS
COLOR: RED
how/what; where/when; who/why; whose/which; how much; how many

NOUNS
COLOR: WHITE
apartment/building; aunt/uncle; baby/babies; ball/doll; banana/watermelon; bathroom/restroom; beach/garden; bedroom/toilet; beer/wine; bird/monkey; birthday/year; book/notebook; boy/girl; broom/bucket; bug/bulb; bus/buses; can/box; candy/candies; car/cars; Carol/Bob; carrot/carrots; cat/dog; cauliflower/cabbage; chalk/eraser; checkers/piano; cheese/ham; chicken/corn; chocolate/sugar; Christmas/Easter; cigarette/candle;

city/bed; coffee/milk; coke/diet coke; cookie/cookies; dad/father; daughter/son; desk/shelf; doctor/nurse; ceiling/floor; door/window; dress/t-shirt; drinks/food; elephant/horse; evening/night; fire/matches; firefighter/driver; flower/rainbow; fruit/vegetables; grandmother/grandfather; hair/mouth; glass/spoon; hand/finger; hat/belt; house/family; ice cream cone/popsicle; January/February; jeans/trousers; juice/water; July/August; kitchen/garage; knapsack/lunchbox; leaf/leaves; lemon/grapes; lion/duck; living room/dining room; magazine/newspaper; man/woman; March/April; May/June; mechanic/engineer; mom/mother; money/clock; morning/afternoon; motorbike/bicycle; November/December; orange/apple; pen/pencil; pie/cake; pineapple/papaya; plate/pan; police officer/pilot; potato/potato chips; radio/tape recorder; rain/river; refrigerator/stove; Saturday/holiday; sauce/mayonnaise; school/classroom; September/October; shoes/socks, shorts/skirt; sister/brother; soap/towel; soft drink/beverage; star/moon; strawberry/pear; Sunday/Monday; supermarket/restaurant; surfboard/skateboard; sweater/bikini; table/chair; tail/cage; teacher/student; telephone/computer; toilet/football; tennis shoes/raincoat; Thursday/Friday; time/watch; tomato/tomatoes; toothbrush/hairbrush

VERBS
COLOR: GREEN
PRESENT
can/must; cook/cooks; come/comes; do/does; brush/brushes; buy/buys; call/calls; jump/jumps; like/likes; listen/listens; live/lives; cut/cuts; dance/dances; don't/doesn't; drink/drinks; drive/drives; eat/eats; give/gives; go/goes; have/has; help/helps; make/makes; open/opens; play/plays; put/puts; read/reads; ride/

rides; mail/mails; sell/sells; sit/sits; sleep/sleeps; speak/speaks; stand/stands; study/studies; swim/swims; take/takes; tape/tapes; travel/travels; walk/walks; want/wants; wash/washes; watch/watches; wear/wears; work/works; write/writes; bring/brings; teach/teaches; understand/understands; sing/sings; think/thinks; there is/there are; there isn't/there aren't; is there/are there; is/'s*; ies/es*; ing/to*; not/n't*; s/n't*; to/ied*; to/ed*; am/'m*; are/'re*; ied/ed*
*half card

PAST/PARTICIPLE
were/been; beat/beat; became/become; began/begun; bent/bent; bit/bitten; blew/blown; broke/broken; brought/brought; built/built; bought/bought; caught/caught; chose/chosen; came/come; cost/cost; cut/cut; did/done; drew/drawn; drank/drunk; drove/driven; ate/eaten; fell/fallen; felt/felt; fought/fought; forgot/forgotten; forgave/forgiven; frozen/frozen; found/found; got/got; kept/kept; knew/known; laid/laid; left/left; lent/lent; led/led; lost/lost; made/made; meant/meant; met/met; paid/paid; put/put; read/read; rode/ridden; rang/rung; rose/risen; ran/run; said/said; saw/seen; sold/sold; sent/sent; shook/shaken; shot/shot; showed/shown; shut/shut; sang/sung; sank/sunk; sat/sat; slept/slept; spoke/spoken; spent/spent; stole/stolen; struck/struck; swam/swum; took/taken; taught/taught; tore/torn; told/told; thought/thought; threw/thrown; understood/understood; wore/worn; won/won; wrote/written; was/been; there was/there were

EXPRESSIONS AND COMMANDS
To be frequently used with the children. Select and balance them in your plans. All levels must deal with them in daily routine, spontaneously and properly.

All these expressions should be always in context.

May I go to the bathroom?; May I wash my hands?; May I drink water?; May I work with…?; May I go out?; May I go to the playground?; May I play with…?; May I draw?; Tie my shoes, please.; I'm hungry.; I'm thirsty.; I don't know.; I want to…; Give me juice, please/thank you.; Give me water, please/thank you.; I love you.; Good morning.; Good afternoon.; Good evening.; Good night.; Good bye.; Hello.; God bless you.; How are you?; How about you?; How are you doing today?; I'm fine, thank you. And you?; I'm pretty good.; I'm bad.; I'm sad.; I'm sick.; Why are you late?; Why are you crying?; How is the weather today?; What day is today?; Did you finish?; What's this/that?; What are you doing?; Look at…; Clean up the table.; Keep all the things.; Keep the games.; Line-up.; What do you want?; Lay down on the floor.; Take off your coat/knapsack/backpack.; Are you sad?; What color is this?; Do you like this?; Do you want this?; For you.; For me.; For us.; Snack.; Lunch.; Rest.; Line.; Thank you.; Give me a kiss.; Free activities.; Music – songs.; Library (book).; Folder.; Sleeping bag.; Notebook.; Bag.; Mat.; Yes, no.; Happy birthday.; Please.; Excuse me.; Congratulations!; It's beautiful.; Sit down.; Stand up.; Sit straight.; Put the things away.; Let's go to the library.; Close the door, please.; Let's…; Shame on you.; Put the chairs under the table.; Pencils in the tin.; Markers in the tin.; Paper to the teacher.; The time is over.; Points.; Bring the material to the teacher.; Help your friend.; Turn on the light, please.; Turn off the light, please.; Pay attention to.; Don't cry.; Join hands.; Shake your hands.; Let's start working.; Jump.; Walk.; Cross your legs.; Hang your coat.; Tip toe.; Come in.; Time is up.; It's time to go home.; Sit down on the line.; Don't shut the door.; Open the door, please.; Wake up.; Clap your hands.; Shake your body.; Stay in your place.; Put your card there.; Get a mat.; Put _____ in your bag.;

Now we have…; Are you ready?; I'm waiting for you.; It's very nice.; Have a nice weekend.; Teacher.; Coordinator.; Agenda/journal/planner.; Odd or even.; Stop doing that.; Open the door, please.; Be quiet.; Screw back.; Flush the toilet.; Wash your hands.; Pull up your sleeve.; Keep going.

- The World into Words – English, a poor or a sophisticated language?

A matter of updating ourselves as teacher

I have been observing the use of English by us while speaking to the students and basic errors are spontaneously done.

The intimate relationship between the SPEAKER and his/her MESSAGE/way of saying something towards the group (the ones who receive the order, the information, the model) is more or less comprehensible according to LINGUISTIC POSSIBILITIES (word knowledge acquisition that can flow spontaneously) we are able to cope with.

Unfortunately, the simple fact of being practicing (talking in English) is NOT ENOUGH to improve competence in English and certainly won't bring the teachers into a more proficient style! On the contrary, some teachers make mistakes which are turned into errors and they are not able to remember what has made them lose the track of their way to say stuff in such a way.

Piaget says: "We can only improve by means of 'Grasp of Consciousness' of what we have done (said) before." So, in order to update our use of English for better ways it is both necessary to be receptive to feedback (do not become ashamed of being corrected or of correcting other people) and to study by our own. DEDICATION is necessary, at least one hour a week and a good dictionary studies/research – especially if you are not very fond of dictionaries nor very disciplined and curious. Be a dictionary wonk! You will be improving your vocabulary repertoire, updating expressions, and being well understood each day. Teachers are supposed to be able to expert in rephrasing their own statements. We should find out other alternatives to say the same thing to reach what students LACK. Their aim is learning and we are there to help them learn.

To make a simpler or a more complex order (instruction) for a Piagetian pedagogical attitude come true, it is not a matter of repetition of what you've said or speaking slower but a matter of skimming in mind a new possibility to rephrase the message. And this should also be done bearing in mind that students should never lose their interest or stop thinking in English. *How could you improve such pedagogical attitude if you are still the same or less proficient language user than you were a month ago?*

# THE SYLLABUS

- *The language at each mental level*

Every language has its own structure, composition and intentions. We must previously define the fundamental dosage of language as a whole. Therefore, we define the point we want to reach at each mental level.

We must consider the capacity and support present at each level in order to understand the universe. As a practical example, we start with the notion of TIME. This notion is linked to the construction of thought based on the fractioning of time which normally occurs in the middle of the concrete-operative level. We now see another that once again will illustrate the issue being dealt with here: the preposition between is an inter-relation of three elements, implying the reversibility of thought and, therefore, only being understood by children after the symbolic period, when this notion is already becoming evident.

Based on these two examples, we have established that:

As a starting point and a syllabus condition, we focused on verb tenses, considering that everything begins with action.

We must always remember that the understanding of a structure in any language antecedes production. Production is expressed firstly through action and, later, through oral means, according to language acquisition criteria.

IMPERATIVE FORM

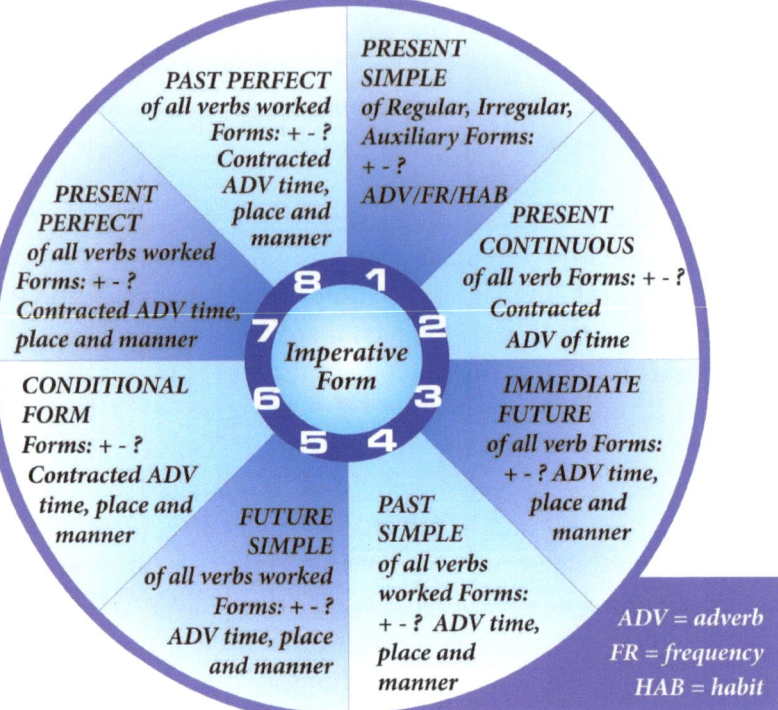

The Imperative Form should be considered the genesis of verb tenses. We require the children to act on "commands"- direct actions, which are practical and concrete-operational, making the best possible use of a number of activities, such as: games, classroom organization, use of material, and so on. This is always done in the form of an invitation, and must not be confused with a demanding, authoritarian or aggressive attitude. Therefore, it is advisable to be as dynamic as possible in regard to the number of verbs without discriminating as to regular, irregular or anomalous.

Based on the time dedicated to verb tenses, we can now dose the other parts of speech that make up the English language. This dosage should be applied according to the needs of use and should bring the context clear, which is intimately linked to the theme being worked. (See The Classification of the Universe).

Attention to the basic rules as to the use of the language:

- Do not save words;
- Overuse speech. Speak and let them speak in the language that is being taught. Every child needs to speak, and it is by speaking they develop the language and experiment thought, with or without a model (under some issue of grammatical need in use);
- Reaffirm what is said, use another structure; do not give the answer to a problem-situation set;
- Make the children discover or invent their own replies; make sure that the problem-situation contains an adequate assimilation scheme;
- Care should be taken to avoid the repetition of a structure with the mere objective of memorization. This does not lead the child to act/think/construct/create/generalize the use of the appropriate language;
- Each child in the group should be offered something new in regard to language structure, despite the supplied model.

CONSIDERATIONS ABOUT:

Colors:
There is no exact moment to highlight some notions, as they should be explored naturally in all units through the use of games, drawings, and more, under orders in graphic representative activities.

Adjectives/Antonyms:
Every notion explored that has a direct and inverse relationship should be worked simultaneously through opposites. Ex: pretty x ugly; small x big, etc. Notions should be constructed from similarities and differences, especially in regard to adjectives. These are relationships: somebody is tall in relation to somebody else that is shorter or less tall. Therefore, students should not be introduced to an adjective without being allowed to examine its relationship with the world.

Numbers and Other Word Classes:
Numbers constitute a very special class. Like colors, they do not have specific moment for exploration. We must bear in mind that this is being constructed from the sensory-motor level and comes to a conclusion at about the intuitive level. To have an idea as to how much something costs or is worth, to have an idea as to how many oranges there are in a total of ten, these examples are all linked to the conservation of numbers. The number genesis is in the correspondence between two elements. The combinatory required for the teaching of reading and writing is linked to the construction of numbers. Finally "counting" correctly only comes about at the age of six/seven years old, at the beginning of the operative-concrete stage. Therefore, learning how to "count" or say the numbers is no real fit up to the age of six. Repeating what is heard in the form of imitation is not necessarily the construction of learning, in many cases. We must be careful not to waste time in our pedagogic activities with concepts that do not permit assimilation schemes wherein the child can deal with a proposed PROBLEM-SITUATION. Check team points in a game played by symbols one by one. By doing this, they will "become aware"of their corresponding level of mental development. As soon as they are able to conserve the number, they themselves will propose to do their own counting of points.

As to conjunctions, generally, it is important to remember that they only begin to form part of a student's life when that student reaches the operatory-concrete level, and is already within the abstract mental stage. Come to a conclusion, predict an attitude, anticipate what is to come are attitudes indicative of abstract thought, mathematical logic. Conjunctions are not taken very far: and, but, and then are used by children.

Language must be used naturally, without any concern for what should or should not be said, so as to avoid the risk of not being understood. We must, however, pay attention to demonstrate by means of actions everything we intend to communicate. It is a great help to exaggerate intonation. Emotions speak, and speak long and loud!

Diversification of the language structure – variations in the way things are said – is an option employed to widen the student's possibilities of understanding. Putting it in another way if, at any given moment, we notice that the student did not heed a given order, the native language should not be used, because by doing this, we are destroying the attempt and effort on the part of the student to solve a problem-situation facing him/her. Hear, understand and obey an order is the problem-situation that forms the basis of acquiring a second language.

- *Adaptation: why suffer to adapt?*

Although adaptation is a very trivial procedure, it is such a hard task or, better saying, a singular and basic step in human's life when debuting in the society. When the obvious is the essential, the essential turns into invisible stuff. Just pure life.

How do we face the world before acquiring the written language? As teachers, we really need to go back to set up the puzzle since the beginning. Since birth!

We are considered teachers, no matter the subject or the level of development we are teaching for, after being able to understand what comes first in mind. What comes before and before the embryogenesis of humanity?

Adapting our students into a new social group is:
– hard but not impossible;
– a notorious attitude but not that unique;
– a matter of awareness for both: student and teacher.

The very young children are still rudimentary. That is why they learn from the general to the specific. But the generic for a child has not the same meaning as for an adult. The sensory motor child learns, acquires, and absorbs a conception or not. It is just a matter of possibility of experiencing.

The "possibles" are not finite and they depend on several circumstances to emerge. Each individual catches up something when the possibilities allow or involve a certain need, a loss or when he/she is wondering too much (to complete other lacks, losses and needs). How can we make sure they are positively learning, acquiring or gaining knowledge? That is the question.

Answering this puzzling issue is as hard as figuring out their point of interest. When they are still sensory they still respond through action. A teacher must be twice emphatic to deal with a child under an active attitude, not yet responding by means of words (because he/she doesn't have them yet and/or because doesn't understand English) and still short spam.

HOW TO BE TWICE EMPHATIC:

Thousands of tips, hints and recipes are not even nearby a reasonable solution because each child behaves uniquely. Below you will find some intuitive tips, but very holistically:

- *Start the activity to organize, do not organize to start.*
- *Start an activity with great enthusiasm, change your tone of voice as much as you can, speak loud, speak low, speak surprisingly, speak funny, and speak silly things, sometimes a word in the native language in the middle of the English structure can help a lot. Nicknames, jokes break the ice. They can possibly smile for a while and that is great.*
- *Stay tuned for each little positive and interested attitude of the ones that are crying (in special). Bearing in mind that the already adapted ones are quite smart is essential. These ones need you to do something that interests them or they will soon start to cry as well.*
- *The sensory motor kids only get adapted when we are smartly able to catch the exact moment in which an activity motivates them. We must try several alternatives to motivate them and avoid crying.*
- *Try to interfere positively into the circular reaction they come through (while this is going on they just cry and don't stop or listen to us at all). Our attitude must "follow the leaders". To be very calm, firm, strong and vigorous; resolute and determined in order to hold his/her attention to us (don't let them run away) with love, kissing him/her for the exact instant that we feel he/she stopped crying even if it is for a minute or two. Take advantage of these moments and advise him/her you are the one who decides in class (it can be in student's native language, if it is more effective – at this point they don't comprehend sentences without action). "You will see mom/granny/nanny as soon as you stop crying". "Mom wants to see you happy, not screaming again". By the way, never forget to honor your promise. As soon as they get into any active initiative, inform the group they will see mom. Be sure he/she won't come back with us spontaneously; once more we must find out another hint to make him/her come back or anyway, he or she should come back to class even crying.*

This is a typical adaptation procedure. It is the first strategy we can take advantage as teachers and coordinators. It works better on the second week, but the problem is that our hearts are too hurt, not only the kids are crying but we suffer with them when they cry. Support when kids are adapting.

There is a way to go. We are the ones to recover because we are the adults. So, take a long breath and relax. Be strong to gain the kid's confidence and also to hold them firmly without hurting them. Don't hesitate, don't be afraid, don't panic and, moreover, don't give up. Just do it and, at the same time, bring good "attacks", good activities. Try to "digitransform" and "digivolve" without moving too much from one place to another. Be sure they will love you too. And you will be rewarded with this level pretty soon.

GOOD "ATTACKS" (SUGGESTIONS):

- *bring balloons to blow in front of them, to eat something they like, drinking water (take a rug to the class), draw them, say their names and yours too; explore each one's English bag or jackets; make a reading game;*
- *record them and make them listen to their voices (together with the teacher's voice);*
- *sing for the very single movements, wash face, comb hair, sit down on the circle, on the chairs, under the table;*
- *sweep or blow their noses (they need to breathe!);*
- *walk around along while (or before) you take them to their families. They should dry the tears more easily and relax before the great encounter;*
- *walk around always singing and talking to them personally. Be careful with wounds or any incidents before they leave. Every little dot is a big reason to cry. They are extremely fragile and they are really suffering, although momentarily. None of their attitudes are*

forever. They cry because they don't know how to deal with the other child, with the new language, with all the new we offer at the moment.
- mix up the good moments with "their moments of suffering";
- be short for each activity;
- quit the activities right on their climaxes;
- vary the most you can, but don't move too much or don't go out of the classroom;
- the body is a reference. Use it.
- make the old ones or the ones that are not crying anymore get involved even more. They should get happy and motivated. Make it more complex for these ones somehow.
- explore your classroom the most and the more basic way you can. They don't know what a crayon is, what paper is, what a chair is, etc. Go step by step.

D. SUGGESTED ACTIVITIES AS PART OF THIS FOLLOWING METHODOLOGY

Basically, our thoughts, when directed towards activities that will work out the language must always be focused on SPEECH. When we are not able to produce a linguistic result with a determined activity, this activity is useless in our pedagogic proposal.

> **IT IS TIME TO...**
> ...LISTEN TO STORIES
> ...SING
> ...PLAY
> ...ACT
> ...DRAW

Therefore, everything employed in relation to a child must be in accordance with the mental level of the child in this group. Whenever possible, we should "say again" when speaking, questioning, relating, dramatizing, emotionally moving the student in order that these different forms of exploration become a part of the didactic resources employed.

The material, space and time available to develop pedagogic practice in an organized activity depend on the teacher, always remembering that we do not intend to create "recipes" or "prefabricated techniques". Everything can be complexified, simplified and generalized.

These are some suggestions, without missing the opportunity to increase the sediment of the practice employed in this methodology. It is important to remember that this method is all about the situation-problem; not only the appropriateness of the situation proposed by the psychopedagogical activity, but also the understanding of the order given in the language being studied. Therefore, the hearing of the announcement of the activity is of the utmost importance in practicing the language under study. The conduct of this activity must be accompanied by SPEECH in the following language, in order to stimulate, question, complexify or simplify, according to each case.

- *Activities with stories*

Generally, stories are used to introduce the vocabulary presented in the unit, especially in regard to sensory-motor, symbolic and intuitive children. With operatory children, we create "situational stories". That is, we develop situations related to the theme (vocabulary) we want to teach during that lesson.

There are a number of ways in which stories are worked. The stories should have a plot, with start, middle and end, and not be a mere description of characters. During the story the teacher should alter his/her tone of voice so as to show suspense, sadness, enthusiasm, anger, thereby helping the child to understand, as the story is being told in the language being worked and also to arouse interest and expectation in the children.

The book, or any other type of material used, must be placed in a way that all children can see it (if not, a loss of interest and disorganization of the group may take place).

STORIES

Together with the audio and visual activity, when students are just observing, we should tell a story with enthusiasm to get them close to a real case.

Here are some suggestions for the variation of working methods in relation to STORY-TELLING:

- listen to stories (use the most varied types of materials

possible: books, puppets, cut-outs, real things, toys, drawings, DVD, and more)
- create your own story to complete the thematic as the main idea of the class
- the different ways to tell a story, using materials variety:

with book on the floor (1)

with book on the chairs

with a kit of elements (2) according to the theme explored

(1) to work in circles promotes the best way for all students to see the teacher, to follow the activity as listening and comprehension.
(2) a kit is a set of elements like toys in general to make the story happen with some real vocabulary.

NOTE: The TELLING of a story depends on the teacher's point of view; attention must be given to the activity from the student's point of view.

- *watch and listen to stories (cartoons, films, books, and more)*
- make up stories
- create a new and different ending to the story
- end a story
- play a game using the story the context as reference for the use of English
- evaluate a story (use a grade for the operatory level students)
- read a story
- complete the story under orders
- write a story
- continue the story with another approach
- draw a story
  - draw a story under orders, drawing and varying the characters or including some other activities along with it
    - speak as one character of a story

These activities fit all levels of mental development and language possibilities.

- more activities and including something else in the page of the story
- paint a story
- color a story
- draw the characters in a story
- create another story using the same characters in the original story
- cut-out and build a story
- prepare a story from scrap and tell the story
- create a story about yourself/your family/etc
- draw a story in chapters
- draw a story in the corner of the paper
- record the story and listen to it
- film the story and watch it
- dramatize the story
- make up a play based on a story
- draw the story in groups/ or paired with a friend
- complete the story with cut-outs
- make a mural of the story using wall posters
- draw the story under the table
- draw the story on the blackboard
- draw the story on the floor
- draw the story on paper having different places (at home, at the zoo, etc)
- build a story with any sort of elements
- build a story under orders
- build a story playing games as a competition
- depict the story using modeling plasticine
- prepare elements taken from the story as requested by the teacher.

ACTIVITIES WITH SONGS

Those teachers who are dedicated to kindergarten school teaching, no doubt have a vast repertoire of infant songs. Children love to sing, and this activity represents an excellent moment for them to express the entire phrasal structure without having to previously structure them in thought. However, the teacher must be careful to make this activity a real moment of learning and not allow it to become a mere question of automatic repetition or mimicry, like that of a parrot. In other to give more richness to the music, the teacher should also take part in the action, in the visual and sentimental presentation. Everything that translates the idea of the lyrics must be worked with the children. Another aspect that should be highlighted in this type of activity is the perfection and drilling of pronunciation. Many times the children are able to pick up the musicality, the rhythm, but repeat unintelligible sounds in a confused burble. Therefore, in order to take care of this point, the teacher should vary this activity as much as possible, introducing a variety of situations. The teacher should also record the students and then let them hear the recording.

It should always be remembered that the music must also accompany the mental level of the children. The teacher should not allow this activity to be omitted from lesson planning. Very often, because of lack of interest in music on the part of the teacher (out of tune or tone death) this happens. This is very unfortunate because by singing the children reach a number of objectives at the same time. So, the teacher should always sing or present the music and let them listen to it.

We now look at some of the activities that add dynamism to songs.

Sing with the teacher

Sing with the CD or mobile phone

Sing with musical instruments

Sing slowly
Sing quickly
Sing loudly
Sing softly
Sing like an elephant (or like any other animal)
Sing while clapping hands

Sing holding a friend's hand
Sing while dancing
Sing silently
Sing for the other group
Sing with mouth closed
Sing backwards
Dramatize the song
Imitate the actions part of the songs
Sing while blocking the nose
Record the children's singing
Sing each part of the song along the class
Complete the lyrics by dictation
Complete the wall posters by drawing the elements that have been left out
Draw the music under orders
Draw the music to make a picture of the song scenario
Improvise the music (film the students singing)
Prepare different lyrics with same rhythm
Make a musical presentation
Imitate what the song says
Sing each part of the song separately (use for generalization of the song lyrics)
Complete the lyrics with cut outs in the form of dictation
Complete the wall posters by drawing the elements that have been left out
Draw the music
Improvise the music (change what the lyric says)
Prepare different lyrics from the same song (good for using unit vocabulary)

Dances (Body Representation):

Musical chairs
Fruit (draw on the floor or prepare large posters containing the objects or words wanted)

Drinks
Means of communication
Circles / Square and other forms (different colors)

Friend at home (a variation of the previous game, in which the remaining student standing answers questions selected by the teacher)

Varied games that can be spoken in the language being taught e.g. Monopoly

Basketball

Skipping the rope

Obstacles

Gymkhana

Survival games

Oral interviews / written interviews / recorded interviews

Blind man's bluff

Handkerchief behind

Tug of war

Kites

Hide and seek

Hopscotch

Statues

Marbles

Graphic acting competitive games

Correspondence games

Note: these games involve the use of language the whole time and also include sections where reading is needed: it is a way to activate reading mechanism. Also, don't forget to illustrate materials.

Games provoke speech. The student involves himself/herself and the points come according to how much the target language is used.

It is important to remember that the Piagetian psychopedagogical activity is based on diversion and dynamic group work. Therefore, we could call all activities used in this methodology (games, competition and challenge, and the rules to be followed by the group) as the soul of this work. We must remember to never allow a child to lose alone – the group wins or loses, never a child individually.

Avoid games that exclude children during the activity ("musical chairs*"as they are played traditionally, for example). What is to be done with these who have been eliminated from the game? Undoubtedly you will end up with only a child under your control and the other will be distracted.

*a game in which players march to music around a row of chairs numbering one less than the players and scramble for seats when the music stops

CREATE AN EXCITING WAY TO OPERATE A GAME SCOREBOARD

Children find scoreboards very attractive. They are able to follow the changes in scoreboard and you have means of maintaining the spirit of the competitive game alive within the group. The teacher should be able to keep the group aware, control the following of the rules between the groups during the activities. It is important that the score be clear and within the understanding of the children. Be careful not to allow the scoreboard to become a register of discipline or grades.

The scoreboard is a means of stimulus, it is not meant to be authoritarian or castrating. It can be used for a number of other student activities, whether by the student to the group or the group to the student. Homework, punctuality, tone of voice and any other rules that arise or become necessary in daily activities. Its value is motivational, and students should take it seriously and trust the teacher not to alter scores. This is important in relation to those who have acquired the ability to conserve numbers (according to the Piagetian theory), very probably, at the intuitive-operatory level and morally, on the basis of an eye for an eye and a tooth for a tooth. Care must be taken not to privilege good students over the others, by giving them advantages. This would take them out of the competition. Create situations in which more advanced students would be permanently under more complex situations, that is to say, challenges; and or simplification for the students who produce less, no matter what the reason is. This is the teacher's role when acting as a referee of the groups.

We suggest, in order to obtain a better understanding of child morals in terms of the Piagetian theory, a reading of some of the bibliography recommendation cited in this material.

REPRESENTATION ACTIVITIES

Before making any suggestions in regard to what should be done to explore representation with children, it is necessary to stress some concepts and remember that activities are not separated, isolated, outside any form of contextualization, but, on the contrary, they should be connected like the links of a chain and securely fastened and closed like a bracelet in brief.

Let's examine the meaning of the word REPRESENTATION:

RE + PRESENT + ACTION this, then, could be understood as show movement in action. The expression itself constitutes movement: SENSORY / MOTOR representation (with the body).

The body action should compose this activity. Starting with imitation as a model, going on to imitation without the model, dramatizing, and then, creating exclusively with the body, the possibility of theater – the interpretive moment with emotional involvement.

The second form of activity suggested will be:

Cronological Range (AGE)	Mental Levels of Development	Moral Development Social Situation	Language Development	Action Representation (1) Graphic (2)	Conservations
From 0 to 2/3 Years Old	Sensory-motor	Anomy Individual	Echolaly Monologue Word Word-phrase	(1)Imitation With Model (2)Scratching/ Cellular/ Fortuite Realism	Permanent Object Construction Semiotic Function Genesis
From 2/3 up to 4/5 Years Old	Symbolic	Floating Pairs Still Anomic	Collective Monologue	(1) Imitation Without Model	Correspondance Collections
From 4/5 up to 6/7 Years Old	Intuitive	Fixed Pairs Genesis of Hereronomy	Adapted Information	(1)Symbolic Games (2)Intellectual Realism Transparency	Substance Number
From 6/8 up to 11/12 Years Old	Concrete Operational	Heteronomy Big Group	Dialogue	(1)Dramatization (2)Visual Realism (respect What Is Not Seen)	Weight Time Volume Length Area
From 11/12 Years Old On	Abstract Operational	Group Autonomy	Discussion (conclusions)	(1)Play (2)Technical Drawing – Drawing In Perspective	Velocity

BRIEFING BOARD
DRAWING/WRITING/TYPING

The levels children go through in regards to representation, are very well detailed.

It must be in mind that it is only possible to represent if the mental image of the object is already constituted. (See chapter on semiotic function).

CHILDREN'S LEARNING CAN ONLY TAKE PLACE BY MEANS OF ACTION

Any language structure aimed must start from effective application = ACTION: do by doing both on the part of the teacher as well as that of the student. (Speech must be accompanied by a demonstration of action, providing a problem-situation which is reported through imitation, dramatization and play).

And, finally, remember that our proposal must always receive maximum priority. We are not scenic art or drawing teachers but teachers of another language.

Therefore, we make use of representation to evaluate the understanding of the students in respect to the language being studied. Any activity that does not bring benefits that develop communication in the language, must be immediately substituted by another that clearly serves to achieve this objective.

Mental Level	Age	Speech Development
Sensory-motor	1 – 2 yo	Echolalia (the senseless repetition of words)
Symbolic/Intuitive	2 – 5 yo	Monologue; collective monologue
Intuitive/Operative	6 – 12 yo	Adapted information; dialogue
Abstract Operatory	12 yo on	Discussion

The steps of speech development according to the Piagetian mental levels of development:

We now look at how representation of action accompanies this speech evolution:

Imitation – when imitating the child generally screams and emits sounds that accompany movements, without bothering to speak. All the children imitate the same thing and do not pay attention to each other (vrum vrum, beep beep, crying and others).

Dramatization – now they repeat the phrases suggested by the teacher and accept the idea that each student is a character in the story, for example: this activity should be proposed at the moment the students are capable of reproducing structures as a whole on the stage, thus making theater feasible. We must not forget that the students need a story activity (object in action) as a model for this activity as dramatization pre-supposes a plot which is needed by the child as a point of reference.

Theater – now the focus is on pre-defined roles, presenting total concern with contextualization / plot and full speech performance.

We suggest, therefore, activities for the practice of action representation:

- Imitate a determined character
- Imitate the teacher
- King of the castle
- Your master ordered
- Speak like your mother
- Walk like a dog
- Take the glasses to the kitchen (carry objects to / from)

- Bath the baby doll
- Walk home (to / from other places)
- Comb hair in front of the mirror (do things in front of the mirror)
- Place things (inside / outside, up / down, behind / in front, etc; explore ideas, topologies, space / object, prepositions)
- Rabbit in the warren (other animals and their habitats)
- Plant beans and water them (plant other things)
- Make vegetable soup
- Make a fruit salad
- Make a cake and put it into the oven
- Cook / prepare other food
- Role on a play
- Different characters
- Imitate a story
- Dramatize the story
- Clap hands while singing the song of the story
- Serve cake
- Arrange / set up the table
- Develop a task
- Go to school
- Swim in the pool at the club
- Climb a tree in the park
- Play with dolls and cars

All the suggested activities are to be always in English. While the children are working with hands they usually speak in the native language. We should be aware and solve this situation with points as in a game as well.

ACTIONS MUST BE EXPLORED USEFULLY/ USE VERBS

According to the main idea of the lesson, the teacher should choose coherent actions and explore them in a sensor/motor manner (acting); symbolically as well; acting symbolically/combining a number of different actions = story; intuitively (acting realistically in a coherent manner and making believe), presenting the product of an action – usefully.

We could remain on this issue for pages and pages, suggesting activities indefinitely. It is important that the teacher clearly understands what this activity consists of, from a linguistic point of view. This activity is based on the dubbing of the vocabulary – structural language universe, apart from constituting an ASSIMILATION SCHEME.

TO KNOW AN OBJECT IT IS NECESSARY TO ACT ON IT.

IN THE BEGINNING, EVERYTHING IS ACTION.

REPRESENTING THE ACTION IS ACTING ON THE OBJECT.

GIVE YOUR STUDENTS ACTIVITIES THAT ARE EFFECTIVELY ACTIVE, NO MATTER WHAT THE ROLE IS.

Matrixes

- Made up of loose leaf pages with drawings representing a context or isolated elements that have to be inserted in the contextualization
- With unit elements (respecting the capacity of each level of development for the number of elements in a page-activity)
- To cut out/color in

- To work individually
- To color in according to instructions
- To complete according to instructions

Constructions

- With scrap (three-dimensional)
- Toy construction with a kit/blocks
- Paper folding games/Making paper figures
- Construct things according to the unit theme

ACTIVITIES SUGGESTIONS

ACTION ACTIVITIES
TO SENSORY-MOTOR/SYMBOLIC LEVELS
ACTING UNDER ORDERS

EXPLORING THE RESEARCH

PLACE THINGS INSIDE

Marquettes

- The city in which we live
- Your suburb
- Your wardrobe
- Your school
- Your school bag
- Your suitcase

We, once again, mentioned that the suggested activities up to now deal with the exploration of kindergarten students' language content, with nothing written yet. We refer here to the audio oral phase. The child up to this point does not yet sing (sensory motor level and starting the contact with the new language, so understands and acts and / or speaks and / or draws).

Graphic representation activities aimed at reading / writing deserve specific treatment. As a child is a human being in development, we often encounter intuitive level groups who are curious about reading or are already reading well their own way in regard to this knowhow. Occasionally they are able to initiate problem-situations arising from reading on their own, depending on the time they have been exposed to the second language. This transitory and introductory period in reading of a second language should be worked with activities there are coherent with what we have proposed up to now. From the kindergarten school period to primary school / intuitive and concrete operatory periods (see characteristics of this level in **Chapter F Part I**), we can only define at this point, distinct treatments in regard to graphic representation activities.

Group A: Students that already communicate in the second language by means of phrasal structures.

Group B: Beginner groups of students in the study of a second language with communication still at isolated vocabulary level.

Students from ***Group B*** are worked under creative problem-situations based on suggestions proposed up to now. We make the best possible use of activities that lead children to construct. In regard to games under rules, these have been found to be highly attractive to them.

Group A students, apart from the increase in oral language structure difficulties, should also be introduced to reading / writing activities. The reading should be based on structures that have already been completely generalized in oral works. There is a slowing down of content in relation to reading; the teacher must make sure that there is no loss of interest by the group in activities aimed at oral development. These groups should proceed with the increase of difficulty during the activities and widening of vocabulary scope. Many times children overestimate reading activities and the teacher inadvertently relegates oral fluency to a lower level of importance. It is at this point in time that oral activities should be more actively worked on, because not all students mature in reading at the same time. This reading activity is just one among so many others.

Graphic representation activities for the specific development of reading: transitory and temporary periods being the construction of language structure on concrete basis.

Explore exhaustively a phrase that defines the class of words in different colors (according to the samples as follows). Apply this material into different games, using them together with a structure as a model. Pay careful attention to the dynamics of this game in order to exemplify the practice of the simple present structure, for example. Each student, depending upon what is to be stressed in the structure, chooses what he or she wants to have, for example, when exchanging a noun in a game of tic-tac-toe. In this way the students discover through a permutation of words in a grammatical class of words how to compose a simple sentence learning its structure at the same time.

Tic-Tac-Toe Game

Work with Third Cards is rich and varied. Everything that is applied in an activity aimed at language structure, the third cards should be presented and their constructions should be requested of the student under dynamic constructivist conditions. This is the best way in which a concrete operatory student will get to know the grammar issues of a language, mixing the grammatical classes within a context, as much as possible. "Becoming aware" should be proposed by the teacher at the same time. Always ask your students to read what they have constructed. Ask the students to make sure that they have really used all the categories that were proposed. Action (Verb), for example, should be considered a fundamental element of the phrase. Therefore, a lack of a color card that corresponds to the action is easily detected when the student reads aloud in group; not only does the group help in becoming aware but, the individual student will perceive that there is something differing from the use of the language. Writing should gestaltically correspond to the structures the student is used to hearing in the fluency of the language under study.

Suggested activities related to graphic representation for the development of writing

- Read and draw / copy the phrase
- Read / cut out / mount and glue phrases (the parts of speech are scrambled, they are in wrong or different positions in the sentences)
- Organize the story sequence
- Search for words (magazines / paper adds / others…)
- Crossword puzzles
- Mixed up letters to discover the words

RESEARCH ACTIVITIES

Research within this methodology is a task that children should take home to do after each class. It is through this activity that the habit of researching is stimulated, thereby widening vocabulary and also keeps parents abreast of what the children are studying during the present. This will also allow parents to stimulate their children to an even greater extent. It is important to remember, however, that the research must be directed at the children and must be done by them in an enthusiastic way. In order to ensure this, the research must be appropriate to their mental level. Thus, research that is either too difficult or too easy will cause the children to lose interest.

The object of research is to widen the student vocabulary and take his or her contact with the subject into home. It is also an opportunity to observe the level of engagement the child has with the language. Research can provide something special in a determined activity, such as, for example, a piece of cloth to be made into a doll, boxes for the construction of means of transportation and / or related to units that have already been worked on. In this case, the degree of difficulty should be gradually increased, starting from action, that is, a real object, until arriving at its representation (photo or drawing of the object). Exemplifying the gradual sequence with the "feeder unit" we would arrive at the following sequence:

1 – Bring a real fruit or a plastic imitation one, if deemed more convenient;
2 – Cut out pictures of fruits of a magazine;
3 – Draw the fruit you like most;
4 – Organize the story sequence
5 – Search for words in magazines, newspapers and so on
6 – Crosswords puzzles
7 – Mixed up letters to discover the word

These activities will never have a 'punishment' aspect. Evaluate the degree of attempts and performance in doing the tasks, never whether it was wrong or right.

SUMMARIZING

The purpose of research is to awaken the child's curiosity, and reach vocabulary and, of course, challenge intelligence. Repetition does not fit this methodology.

COPYING

Copying of a word from a dictionary into an appropriate space. (From a sentence that the group has formed for a game, from a friend's work, from a wrapper, from a magazine, etc.) It is necessary for graphic organization of writing. Therefore, this stage must be allowed, for it is fundamental. Do not stop or censure them for this. Promote activities that stimulate this type of activity.

WRITING INCORRECTLY

Allow the students to write whatever they want to and/or feel they need to in any way they can. No doubt they will make use of their mother language phonetic system as it is already acquired and so, stronger. Do not correct or criticize them for this. Ask the students to read what they have written. In this way there will be no confrontation with the 'error' and there will be a much greater production on the part of the students in this activity. The 'correction' of these 'errors' in writing will, gradually, be corrected by the activities aimed at reading. 'Becoming aware' occurs during the process of reading as well as writing activities.

READING OF STORIES

Plan the reading of stories from story books for your students even though they don't have all the vocabulary content for reading, they must be brought into contact with it in a spontaneous way. Reading is to provide one with pleasure. Reading about a theme that is of interest of the students is much more lively and stimulating than dealing with a cold text in the form of a booklet where there is no student involvement. Stimulate reading and help them in this task.

Newspapers and magazines in English only should form part of student reading material. Cut out items that they already know how to read; extracting from context promotes special stimulus, making reading useful. Join words, product of this research, and use them in the preparation of phrases, stories, murals, and classify them into grammatical categories.

When working with the coloring in of a drawing, for example, we can insert elements, cut out or color many others, depending on the greater or lesser exposure to the language each of the students has.

We suggest therefore that this activity be followed in the widest possible generic way, leaving the teacher's responsibility for creativity open to excellent opportunities in regard to graphic representation. These tasks can be applied under individual and or group's solicitation.

MURALS

With loose elements so as to include contextually in a scene and to promote the group work:

- Shadow
- To color in according to instructions (teacher's orders)
- To draw in what is missing according to teacher's instructions
- Lyrics to complete
- Notices to be organized in sentences in an appropriate sequence
- Wall newspapers
- Product advertisings
- Sticking elements under orders

DRAWING

- Of a story under orders
- Of a song
- Of elements under orders
- Of phrases spoken by the teacher
- Group against group (order given x order given)
- On different types and shapes of paper

Here are some suggestions for research related to the mental level of the children:

SENSORY/MOTOR/SYMBOLIC

The research must be as concrete as possible: toys, items of clothing, things to eat and to drink, photos and more.

SYMBOLIC/INTUITIVE

Apart from photographs and real objects, drawings, magazine and newspaper cut-outs can also be requested. The number of things may be limited. For example, cut-out an element for each finger of one hand, a hand of things (a basis of five) from those who know the names of the things in English.

INTUITIVE/OPERATORY (WITHOUT WRITING YET)

The same things required from symbolic/intuitive children can be requested for these levels but implement more elements in the activity.

The form of exploration, however, is different; the degree of performance may be increased or made more difficult. Children can also be asked for things that they do not altogether know yet, for example a recording of music sung in English or an imported article, thereby stimulating the child to search within his/her universe for things from the most varied of origins, remembering to contextualize so that not only the name of the object is explored, but its use as well.

OPERATORY (WITH WRITING)

A child can be asked to cut out words in English, look up words in a dictionary or bring books or magazines written in English to the classroom.

Puzzles, jigsaws, and other activities from the intuitive level constitute an attractive task for children at operatory levels; the work is stimulating and indispensable.

Crossword puzzles are considered a form of home research. Jigsaw puzzles are entertaining activities which explore the level of mental development of the child and, at the same time, indicate creative capacity.

Evaluate the means employed by the children to resolve problem situations proposed and not the results.

Children who become accustomed to doing research incorporate a very high 'scientific' attitude, which will be of great utility in the professional field in later life. The world requires creative people in ever-growing numbers.

Some tips of activities for very, very young learners

The sensory-motor's level of comprehension of the world (the toddler's reality only and mainly) is through the action.

The action coming from their body movement and all the discoveries' starting points are founded on their own bodies. They are not yet prepared for pretending or imaginative activities.

Focus on the main object of studies: do not forget to say what you do and do what you say. They will not be able to reproduce orally at first, but perform under teacher's models.

Videos, video clips, sing along, stories with kits, exploiting an object for no longer than 5 minutes are examples of activities that may work. Although they can be repeated more than once in the same class, they can't stand any longer than very short time concentration.

The more you vary, the more engaged they get.

Always have this in mind: they pay more attention to human than to the mechanical sounds reproduction.

Focus on their mental level: basically the state of moving all around is important.

Thus, some verbs/actions that may work are: to come x to go, to hold (hands, bags, cups), to clap hands, to stamp (the feet somewhere), to hold (something, someone's hand, teacher's pants, a hook, a rope), to walk, to move around, to go to another place, to dance, to carry and bring, to put (something on, under, in, out, at), to wrap, to unwrap, to jump, to skip, to tweet, to move, to pull x to push, to close x to open, to tear, to clean, to gather.

Focus on the materials: pool table, basic table, floor, salon, cars, street, blue carpet indoors, black carpet for outside activities, balls, pails, big kit elements. Space out the material, never leaving them unassisted (nor the kids!). Remove distraction. Using objects and then keeping them away is the best strategy. Create an environment to each context under each material. Decentralizing from the one being used helps to engage on the next one. Then, while proposing the next activity, collect the material that has just been used.

Crayons are the only scribbling material for this level. Fixed papers on the table work better.

GAMES:

Peek-a-boo; hide and seek, placing pieces, car racing, and battery toys, catching the teacher, monkey says and never forgetting the oral use of English during the activities.

SONGS:

No matter the action you are proposing, for repetition somehow, make it up into a pleasant song or rhymes. Change voices, strong or low, play sounds, make listening fun.

Youngsters need to hear the same words many times. Use lots of gestures; express yourself through your face. Talk facing your audience. Create funny sounds to mimic sounds, to talk to the students and more.

E TECHNIQUES AND ADVICE FOR THE TEACHER TOWARDS STUDENTS' DYNAMICS

Start to organize instead of organizing to start

The teacher should start his/her activity by allowing the students to perceive what is happening. In the case of games, for example, it is not necessary to explain how they work: only by playing will the children understand the mechanism and rules of the game.

When frying fish, chase the cat away

The teacher must keep the objective in mind, keep within the time limits set aside for the game and also, observe those students who are not totally interested in the activity; simplify for some and increase the degree of difficulty for others, demonstrate while speaking; be the referee/umpire of the game; arrange seating around the book and continue the story. In fact, 'without jumping into the pool' with the students, maintain a view of the whole group. It is the teacher who directs the show (the classroom).

It is time for… / Time is up or over

Do not abuse the period of concentration, do not overwork the activity. Even when the group is engaged in the activity, time limits must be set by the teacher so that there is no reduction in interest.

Insist upon the group facing you when you give an order. The teacher must show what he/she is saying with actions, so that the whole group obeys the order given.

The latecomer

Receiving and introducing a child to an activity that is already in progress is an immediate attitude. The child is not to blame for coming late to class; he/she should be welcomed by the teacher who should thereupon summarize what is happening and, if necessary, introduce the child to the task until the child feels completely at ease.

The difference between understanding an order and obeying it

The teacher should, when giving an order to the group, observe how the students react in relation to execution of the task. There are children who do not start immediately because they have not understood the order (this then represents a problem-situation), whether from the point of view of the action itself, or because of a linguistic point of view. The teacher, in this case, should try another approach so that the student takes part in the activity. If the teacher sees a failure to obey arises from disorganization, the students should be dealt with individually, checking if there is a need to simplify or increase the degree of difficulty in respect to order given, as a means to recover student's interest in the activity.

The class is in a state of uproar. Now what?

The teacher should not become disturbed when a group does not achieve the expected objective in a determined activity. Do not let the group decide what is going to happen next. Normally, when an order given does not correspond to the intellectual level of the students, the result will be disorder and chaos. Change the order, or even the activity as a whole; do not be influenced or carried away by the disobedience of the group or by loss of emotional control displayed by the students

The teacher has to overcome the situation, even if the activity is cancelled and another is started. A child needs the order given by a "chief". Until the end of the concrete/operatory level, heteronomy is their organizational form, so, asking them what they would like to do will only disrupt the group because only the abstract operatories are capable of reaching a stage of autonomy. This attitude generates total insecurity in the group, leading to "chaos". So, it is the teacher's duty and responsibility to normalize the situation in any didactic circumstance. The teacher should "calm down" the group with another activity; it is no use asking for silence. It is useful to have an "ace up the sleeve", an activity that the teacher is confident in using. Games and music are a great help. Do not let the group break up. Gently take hold of them immediately and get them working on the activity. Once one activity has been concluded, the next must be announced immediately, remembering that the arrangement of the classroom is also an activity. Example: papers or pieces of objects should be given back to the teacher; chairs under the table, pencils in their boxes; sit in a circle, etc.

*take advantage of organizational moments to set points as in a game

"Correction": what is right and what is wrong

The teacher should see errors committed by children as being caused by the absence of a scheme to solve the question. Check what was omitted during the progress of the activity and go back to the point where the child is able to answer a question put in a phrasal structure. If there is still no communication use isolated words. This is the scheme he/she will use.

A CHILD CAN ONLY CARRY OUT AN EXISTING TASK THAT IS WITHIN HIS/HER COMPETENCE. (L.O.L.)

- *What do you do if a child attending an English class uses his or her native language the whole time?*

It is important to make it clear that collective monologue is very strong among them; in the same way that they speak, they do not wait for an answer, and we become very anguished in proposing a foreign language and the native language predominates. We must, very quickly, evaluate the reasons that lead a group or a child to speak in the native language.

- *I don't care if I lose a point!*
Do not allow any student to withdraw from the game; he/she must be kept in the competition the whole time. There must be something he or she is good at.

- *The balance between criticism and praise*
This search must be constant, both in regard to the student individually or in group and in respect of one group and another. Do not only criticize nor only praise – balance this formula of success.

- *I think they do not like me*
  Am I being difficult?
  Am I being disagreeable?
  I don't like this group.
  This group has a difficult student.

We must work with the whole ox; a group of students, no matter what it is made up of, it is a unit. In using an ox as a comparison, an entire ox: if we remove a kidney from the ox the other kidney becomes stronger and takes over the function of the one removed so that the ox can continue to survive. This process takes place in a group: if what we consider to be a problem leaves the group, another will take its place so that the group will continue to exist.

THE WHOLE CONTAINS WHAT THE PARTS DO NOT.

Do not cut up the group; make use of each element. All the parts have their essential functions. And on the other hand, our group of children is our mirror image. Evaluate the fact whether, for the group, there is a need for emotion and tonus. We can use as a sample: "worth what we weigh"; if we perform our role satisfactorily, we are liked by the students; if we fail more than we succeed, we are boring teachers. However, as soon as we recover our forces, the children start to love us. Just like a chameleon that changes its color to protect itself in dangerous situations, a child reacts immediately when a teacher overdoses the structural sequence of this psychopedagogical proposal.

Concluding this chapter, which appears to be very much like a patchwork quilt, we must always bear in mind that AN ALL ENCOMPASSING VIEW is fundamental in the work of an EDUCATOR. A child may, in the end, lose contact with an adult, but an adult must never lose touch with the child. This is basic advice to be followed at all times and under any circumstances.

*E*VALUATION OF THE STUDENTS IN TERMS OF THE CLINICAL METHOD

In evaluating a student, the teacher must consider the psycho-emotional behavior, the performance of the student and the relationship towards the teacher, other students and with the structures of the language under study. After all, the proposal of this methodology goes very far beyond the simple fixation of content. It aims at the intellectual development of the individual, that is, it is concerned with intellectual, socio-cultural and moral growth of the student. Therefore, the teacher must evaluate the student in respect to various aspects, taking into consideration the objectives that are being endeavored to reach in each of the activities proposed.

Items to be observed and evaluated by the teacher:

Adaptation process
How the student adapts to an activity and to the group; if the student cried or not; if help was needed.

Interest
Whether the student shows interest or not for the language under study or if there should be interest, it is irregular.

Attendance
Whether the student is assiduous or there are many absences along the period, whether the student is punctual or normally comes late for class.

Participation
Whether the student participates in proposed activities with tonus or not. What activity the student likes best.

Orders

Whether the student understands orders given in English, easily or not. Whether he/she obeys them with alacrity or not.

Cooperation

Whether the student cooperates with group work, helps friends, or only does things on being asked to do so, by the teacher.

Pronunciation

Whether it is clear or still confusing or with native language accent.

Tone of voice

Whether it is low, audible or very loud.

Research

Whether the student always accomplishes the requested research, whether the student never brings it or bring it sometimes.

Reading and writing

This item is evaluated only in regard to students who have started the process. The teacher must take into consideration the fact that the student forms phrases easily and spontaneously, whether words are written with easy or whether words are still copied, whether texts can be read, etc.

The teacher should determine the percentage from = 0% to 100% what the student is able to achieve in a period. All the content worked in a period is considered as being 100%. Each student reached a part of this percentage.

However, the objectives established in each activity proposed should be transformed into items to be observed in the student. For example, when they are singing, the teacher should observe their tone of voice, if they like the activity or if someone participates timidly.

Through these observations, the school report is prepared. Therefore this document assumes great importance as far as the student is concerned. It is pertinent for the teacher to inform parents of the global development of the child and register this information so as to improve the work and define the situation for the next period. This is what a school report consists of.

Register the facts as a matter of routine in your professional life. Do not depreciate occurrences in the classroom or in regard to students individually; there is no doubt you will not remember all the details of situations experienced with the passing of time.

STUDENT EVALUATION SAMPLE

I – HABITS

Assiduity:
Attendance and punctuality
Classes given: _____ Number of absences: _____
Reason: _____

Punctuality
Arrives and leaves on time
Usually arrives late
Sporadically arrives late

Use of material
Careful in handling
Satisfactory organizes at the end of the activity
Organizes when asked to by teacher
Disorganized: destroys
Mixes up in a disorganized way
Puts materials in mouth
Tears materials

Practical work: use of material
Uses scissors with ability
With difficulty
Does not know how to use scissors
Uses paint brushes and pens with ability
With difficulty
Damages
Uses glue and paint in general
Refuses to participate
Adequate use
Disorganized
Makes physical experiences with material

English personal material
Systematically brings it
Is careful
Rarely brings it
Badly looked after
It is forgotten
Usually accompanied by parents
Lost
Was substituted during the period

Research
All done
Done by third parties
Delivered enthusiastically when arriving
Doesn't know if it was done
Rarely done
Never brings it
Shares well with some group

Puzzles
All done
Shows interest
Shows difficulty in understanding

II – GENERAL ORGANIZATION

In a circle (in group)
Occupies a place well
Stays in place
Prefers to be at teacher's side

Graphic representation activities (at table)
Individually
Is organized
Is becoming organized
Easily disorganized
Obeys orders given

In group
Cooperates with the group
Performs part without provoking group
Integrates well
Refuses to work in group

III – SOCIALIZATION

Adaptation process
Completely adapted
Adapted very well
Cried during adaptation
Needed a special scheme for team adaptation
Needed a parent in the classroom

Arrival at class
Excited
Come to the team alone
Did not want to join in
Wanted the company of parent until entered classroom

CONCLUSION

One of our main goals is to make sure students are able to take regular classes in schools in which the official language is English, thereby being able to practice oral and written communication under total immersion conditions.

We must first evaluate the differentiated intention of this Methodology to educate in school, starting from a change in the view of education. The teacher then is able to break through the barrier created by form and inform, clearly dosing, without interruption, the study objective.

The most difficult task in education is to LINK the study objective to the study itself.

BIBLIOGRAPHY

CHOMSKY, Noam. *Linguagem e mente*. São Paulo: UNESP, 2009.

CHOMSKY, *Syntactic Structures*. New York: Mouton, 2002.

LIMA, Adriana Flávia S. O. *Pré-Escola e Alfabetização: Uma proposta baseada em Paulo Freire e J. Piaget*. Petrópolis: Vozes, 1986.

LIMA, Lauro de Oliveira & LIMA, Ana Elizabeth de Oliveira. Uma escola *piagetiana*. Rio de Janeiro: Paideia, 1983.

LIMA, Lauro de Oliveira. *A construção do homem segundo Piaget: Uma teoria da educação*. São Paulo: Summus, 1984.

LIMA, Lauro de Oliveira. *Mutações em educação segundo McLuhan*. São Paulo: Summus, 1980.

LIMA, Lauro de Oliveira. *Piaget para Principiantes*. São Paulo: Summs, 1984.

PIAGET, Jean & INHELDER. B. *A psicologia da criança*. Rio de Janeiro: Fundo de Cultura, 1973.

PIAGET, Jean. *A linguagem e o pensamento da criança*. Rio de Janeiro: Fundo de Cultura, 1973.

PIAGET, Jean. *A psicologia da inteligência*. Rio de Janeiro: Zahar, 1977.

PIAGET, Jean. *O juízo moral na criança*. São Paulo: Summus, 1994.

PIAGET, Jean. *Para onde vai a educação*. Rio de Janeiro: José Olympio, 1978.

PIAGET, Jean. *Psicologia e pedagogia*. Rio de Janeiro: Forense, 2015.

PIAGET, Jean. *Seis estudos de psicologia*. Rio de Janeiro: Forense, 1972.

RICHARDS, J. & ROGERS, T. Chapters I & II in: *Approaches and Methods in Language Teaching:* Cambridge University Press, 1986.

RICHARDS. J. *"The Secret Life of Methods"* in: TESOL. Quaterly 18 (1), 1984.